No. 1724
$19.95

how to
DOCUMENT YOUR SOFTWARE

by barbara spear

TAB BOOKS Inc.
BLUE RIDGE SUMMIT, PA. 17214

To Corky,

You've always been around to catch me when I fall.
You've given me the freedom to do what I must do.
You're the eye in my hurricane, my refuge from the storm.
You're my rock of Gibralter; my beacon in the fog.
You're a mountain man with gentle ways and a love for the simple life.
You're my husband and my best friend. I love you.

06-10157602

FIRST EDITION

FIRST PRINTING

Copyright © 1984 by TAB BOOKS Inc.

Printed in the United States of America

Library of Congress Cataloging in Publication Data

Spear, Barbara.
How to document your software.

Includes index.
1. Electronic data processing documentation.
I. Title.
QA76.9.D6S64   1984   001.64'2   83-18108
ISBN 0-8306-0724-2
ISBN 0-8306-1724-8 (pbk.)

Contents

Introduction

The market for home computers is exploding. Every day new computers are introduced that are smaller, more powerful, and cheaper than ever before. As a result, the profile of the computer owner is changing rapidly. For many years, the people who owned computers were people who were interested in programming. This is no longer true. The new breed of home computer owners often has little experience or interest in programming.

In part, this transition is due to the increased number of word processing programs that are available. Another factor is the use of computer assisted instruction in schools. Parents are beginning to feel that their children need a computer at home today as much as they needed a calculator five years ago. Finally, with the ever increasing pace at which we live, many people have discovered that a computer can save them time, a precious commodity.

The new breed of home computer owners wants easy-to-use, prepackaged programs. They're looking for programs that they can drop into their system and run with little or no modifications. This has opened up a gigantic market for original programs. Because the need for useful, reasonably priced software exceeds the current supply, you don't have to be "somebody" to write and sell programs. Many of the best programs available today were written by self-taught programmers just like you.

The biggest problem with home-written programs is the documentation—or lack thereof. Most self-taught programmers do not know how to write documentation. Many don't see a need for spending the time it would take to document their programs. In the past, home programmers were a tightly knit group. Minimal documentation and sketchy flowcharts were accepted by fellow programmers partially because nobody really knew how to write documentation, and partially because the programmers had the skills necessary to read and interpret the actual code.

The business and scientific worlds have always insisted on complete, accurate program documentation. The programming languages used by these professionals have highly standardized formats and conventions for preparing documentation. The methods and techniques for preparing such documentation are taught in schools throughout the country.

Unfortunately, languages like FORTRAN and COBOL are not widely used on home computers. The processing logic and methodology they use and its corresponding documentation are not directly transferable to BASIC, the most popular language for home computers.

For many years BASIC has been looked down upon by educators and data processing professionals. It has often been referred to as a language for "babies and hackers." Because of this negative stigma, few courses in BASIC have been offered. Those courses that have been available have focused on coding syntax and techniques, not documentation.

Where, then, was the BASIC programmer to turn for guidance when it came to documentation? It seemed a shame that the best sources available gave guidance for documenting programs written in other languages. Moreover, the documentation they described was intended for a formal, professional, and captive audience. The people who read giant tomes of COBOL or FORTRAN documentation usually had little choice; it was part of their job or professional responsibility. Long-winded, stuffy text was tolerated and came to be a routine part of the standard manual.

Having waded through many such manuals, I decided to stage an individual revolt against such boring text. I wanted my documentation to be both useful and enjoyable to read. My efforts were rewarded. The documentation I wrote was often described as easy-to-follow, readable, and useful.

I spent a lot of time teaching workers how to use new systems their company had purchased. This gave me good insights as to the kinds of things users want and need to know. I became conscious of a distinct contrast between my teaching techniques and those of programmers. In most cases, the programmers either rushed through the material at lightning speed, or spent hours describing the neat programming techniques they'd used. This left the users more confused and anxious about the system than they had been before "training."

I decided to write this book because of my sincere commitment to John and Jane Q. User. I felt that they were being short-changed by much of the documentation currently available. In many instances, programmers expressed an honest desire to produce a quality product. The problem was that they didn't know how to go about it.

Many programmers have a limited understanding of what their users want and need to know. They don't recognize the difference between audiences and don't know how to tailor documentation to a specific audience. Moreover, many programmers feel uncomfortable as writers. They're not confident about their written communications skills.

This book was written to show programmers how to document their work. Many long hours go into designing, coding, and testing a program. With this book as a tool, the programmer can now accompany a well-written program with quality documentation.

ACKNOWLEDGMENTS

I would like to thank Coleco Industries, Inc. for letting me reprint the Super Action™ Baseball booklet. Special thanks should also go to ADAM® because I prepared the entire manuscript on my ADAM computer. My agent Bill Dunkerley, my husband Charlie, the editor Marilyn Johnson, and my friends and coworkers deserve special appreciation for being patient and understanding while this book was being written.

Chapter 1

The Need for Documentation

The term documentation usually calls up visions of pages upon pages of text written in stuffy, hard-to-follow technical jargon. The illustrations that accompany this text are frequently complicated and filled with cryptic symbols.

While this description may fit some documentation, it certainly doesn't accurately describe it all. Moreover, it is by no means necessary for documentation to be stuffy, hard to follow, or cryptic. In fact, when documentation is difficult to read and understand, it defeats its own purpose.

Documentation is a way of explaining what your programs do, how they relate to one another, and how they work. It is an important functional element of any software program or system you write. It is documentation that helps you figure out how to use a new system, how to troubleshoot logic errors, and how to customize or adapt a program so it meets your special needs.

HOW IS DOCUMENTATION USED?

Documentation is used as a reference tool throughout the life cycle of a program or system of programs. It is used during the initial development phase, during the operational phase, and during the maintenance phase.

When a program or system of programs is being developed, documentation provides a guide for programmers and designers. It shows them how the program or system should work and what it is being designed to do. Specifications are a form of documentation. They tell a designer or programmer what tasks each program should perform and what limitations, restrictions, and considerations must be taken into account by the code. Flowcharts show the information path through a program or system of programs. They make the designers and programmers aware of what information must be available at various processing points within each

1

program. Logic lists are used to develop the actual processing steps within a program or subroutine. Pseudocode is used to test coding ideas. It lets programmers "walk through" the processing sequence for a program or subroutine without burdening him with the syntax restrictions of actual code.

There are other types of documentation that are used by designers, analysts, and development programmers; but all serve the same purpose. They direct the user towards a specific goal. The software is being designed to perform a task. The documentation identifies the task and indicates the processing method that should be used to accomplish that task.

After a program is coded and has been tested successfully, it can be put into production. This means that the program can be put to work doing the job for which it was designed.

During the operational phase of a program, documentation serves as a set of instructions or a reference manual. It shows users how to run the program and how to handle exception conditions. If the program requires external information or responses to questions, the documentation indicates what kind of data the program needs, and what the program considers to be valid responses to its questions.

After a program has been used for a while, it sometimes needs to be changed. In some cases, the way in which the program is used changes. At other times, enhancements are added to the original design. Enhancements may add new capabilities to a program, or may simply improve the speed and performance of a program. Sometimes, little bugs that escaped notice during the original workability testing are discovered and must be corrected.

Regardless of why a program is being modified, one thing is critical: before a change can be made, it is essential to understand how the program works. It is also helpful to know how the program was originally intended to work. Access to detailed documentation of this kind is a rare luxury.

The most direct and readily available form of documentation that is used during the maintenance phase is the program listing. This is usually a printed copy of the actual lines of code that make up the program. A listing can be studied by a maintenance programmer to determine where within the code certain operations are performed. Notations can be made on the printed sheets indicating where changes should be inserted and what the coding changes should be.

Documentation is an important reference tool during every phase in the life cycle of a program. Unfortunately, useful documentation is a scarce commodity. It isn't available when it's needed. If documentation is available, the odds are that it is sketchy and incomplete, out of date, and inaccurate.

WHO SHOULD WRITE DOCUMENTATION?

Documentation should be written by technical writers, right? Wrong!

Anyone who writes a program has prepared a form of documentation. As mentioned previously, program listings are often used by maintenance programmers as their sole source of information for determining how a program works.

Documentation can be prepared by analysts, designers, programmers, or technical writers. The important thing is not who writes the documentation, but that it gets written, is technically accurate, and is helpful.

Because documentation takes on many forms, it isn't necessary to be a brilliant writer in order to prepare documentation. Often a neatly drawn flowchart provides a more useful reference than 100 pages of text.

IS DOCUMENTATION REALLY NECESSARY?

The answer is emphatically YES! Documentation keeps a programmer on course while developing and coding a program. It reminds him of all the restrictions, considerations, and conditions that must be taken into account by the program. Documentation teaches a new user how to properly run a program. Documentation explains the processing and logic of a program to a maintenance programmer who wants to modify or customize the code.

But what if the programmer who designed and wrote the program is the only person who will use it? This would be a very rare occurrence. If a program performs a useful task or contains a well written subroutine, the temptation to share the program with a friend or fellow member of a Users' Group is almost irresistable. However, if the program is used solely by the programmer that designed and wrote it, there is still a need for documentation.

Lets say you write a dozen programs in a year. That's about one a month. Each program contains one or more special, efficient subroutines that you spent a lot of time designing and are rather proud of. You'll probably find that you use some of your programs all the time, and others are used only occasionally. After writing a dozen programs, you'll find if difficult to remember how to use some of the programs that you run only once in a while. After a couple of years, you'll probably find that not only can't you remember how to run some programs, but you can't remember which programs contain which subroutines. When you're ready to write a detailed program that requires processing logic that you've already worked through, it is fast and safe to copy the code from an existing program and modify it to suit the needs of your new program. If you have neglected to document your progams accurately you may find it difficult (if not impossible) to locate the subroutines you need. If you don't know where to find the code, you must reinvent it. This wastes both design and testing time. If you need to modify one of your early programs, you'll have to waste time reacquainting yourself with the logic and the code before you can attempt to make changes.

Here's one last thought on the necessity of documentation. The software industry is growing rapidly. New inexpensive computers are being introduced all the time. The purchasers of these computers are often average folk who want a computer that can help them with everyday tasks. Many new computer owners don't have the talents or interest in developing original programs. They want to purchase a program that they can drop into their computer and run with a minimal effort on their part. Many hobbyists have discovered that there is a demand for the programs they write. Noncoders are willing to pay for useful, working programs that meet their needs. These users insist, however, that the programs be accompanied by helpful, easy-to read documentation. If you're writing programs, you can make a lot of money; but you'll have to provide your customers with useful, quality documentation.

Chapter 2

Who Uses Documentation?

Everyone involved with computers, programming and data processing uses documentation. Documentation provides the key you need to unlock the secrets of programming logic and to use a program with maximum efficiency.

DOCUMENTATION FOR DESIGNERS

Program developers are people who recognize a problem that can be solved using a computer. They study the problem. They determine the sequence in which the computer will perform the tasks that will solve the problem. They write code that tells the computer how to solve the problem. They test the code to see if it works the way they thought it would. Finally, they have a finished program that solves a problem and performs useful tasks.

How does a designer make the transition from recognizing a problem and creating a program to solve it? He uses documentation. Sometimes a de-

signer keeps documentation in his head. This can be risky and frequently leads to careless logic and coding errors. These errors often show up in preliminary testing, and the end result is unnecessary and avoidable recoding.

You can avoid a lot of mistakes when you design programs if you write things down as you go along. First, write a problem statement. This is a detailed description of the problem you want to solve. You need to be very specific and note every aspect of the problem so that you won't forget anything later. Figure 2-1 shows an example of the type of problem statement you might write down. Note the amount of detail that is included.

After you've clearly identified the problem, it's time to divide your work into manageable pieces. To do this, you divide the solution of the problem into tasks. If you are designing a complete system, such as an accounts payable system, each of the tasks might represent a module or program within

Voucher Entry Program

This program will accept data from invoices and statements that are received from vendors and incorporate the information into the accounts payable system for payment.

The operator will enter a vendor code. which will be validated against the master vendor file. If the code matches an existing code. the rest of the information can be processed. If there is no match. a new vendor record must be created before processing can continue.

The operator will enter the date of the invoice or statement. This date is validated against a date routine for numeric accuracy only.

The operator will enter an invoice total. This amount is either manually calculated prior to data entry or is read from a total at the bottom of the input document.

The operator will enter line amounts for all items on the document. These amounts will be accumulated as they are entered. When the operator has entered all the amounts. he will type DONE. The accumulated total will be compared against the operator entered batch total. If the two amounts are equal. processing will continue. If they are not equal, a message will flash at the bottom of the screen saying TOTALS DO NOT MATCH. The message will remain until the operator types the word DONE again. The operator may type-over any line amounts or type-over the word DONE to add additional line amounts. The space bar will permit erasure of any unwanted line amounts.

When all entries have been made, the operator will type the word END instead of a vendor code. The program will then write voucher records into the master accounts payable file for each vendor and prepare a voucher entry summary report. This report will list the vendors (in the order in which they were entered), the detailed line amounts, and the total. A grand total will be printed at the end of the report.

Fig. 2-1. This is a problem statement for the Voucher Entry program in an accounts payable system. It describes how the vouchers will be entered, what validations are necessary, what information is required, how to handle problem situations, and what information must be passed to other files/programs in the system.

the system. The tasks within each program will represent the subroutines you will need to make the program work. The number of tasks you identify will depend upon the size and complexity of the problem you're trying to solve.

You can use a block diagram or flowchart to show graphically how the tasks fit together to solve the problem. It's like a jigsaw puzzle. Each of the tasks represents a piece of the puzzle. When you put them together correctly, you have a pretty picture (or in the case of programming, a solved problem).

Figure 2-2 shows a sample block diagram. It identifies each task by name, but it doesn't show the

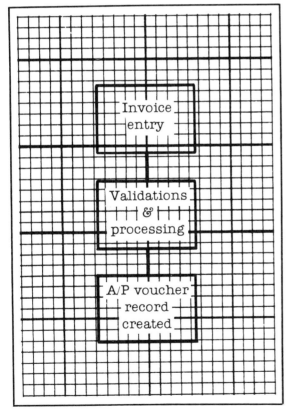

Fig. 2-2. This is a block diagram for the Voucher Entry program.

information flow or processing sequence within each task. Once you've identified the tasks that make up the pieces of your programming jigsaw puzzle, you can shift them around until they're in the proper order. If the tasks don't work together correctly when you put them in one sequence, switch them around until the problem is solved. (If you're drawing a block diagram, a pencil and large eraser are essential tools because they let you experiment and change your mind easily.)

Each task will involve several processing steps. You can illustrate the order in which these steps should be performed using a traditional flowchart. Your flowchart will show the normal information flow and how the processing handles exception conditions. When you draw a flowchart, you have the opportunity to visually walk through the logical processing steps that must be taken to complete each task. Naturally, these steps must be taken in the proper sequence, or they'll never complete the task. By drawing the flowchart, you begin to think about the order in which you must take the necessary steps. You can experiment with that order until you've taken care of all the restrictions and conditions that may throw roadblocks in the way of getting the task accomplished. Figure 2-3 shows a flowchart for one of the tasks shown in the block diagram.

After you've written a problem statement and prepared some block diagrams and/or flowcharts, you're ready to tackle some of the nuts and bolts coding decisions. At this point, some programmers jump head first into coding. A safer transitional step is to write some *pseudocode*. Pseudocode lets you verbally map out the processing without worrying about adhering to the rules and regulations of coding. Pseudocode is especially helpful to machine-language programmers because the actual lines of code are often more cryptic than code lines in high-level languages like BASIC. Figure 2-4 shows a sample of pseudocode.

The preliminary documentation helps the de-

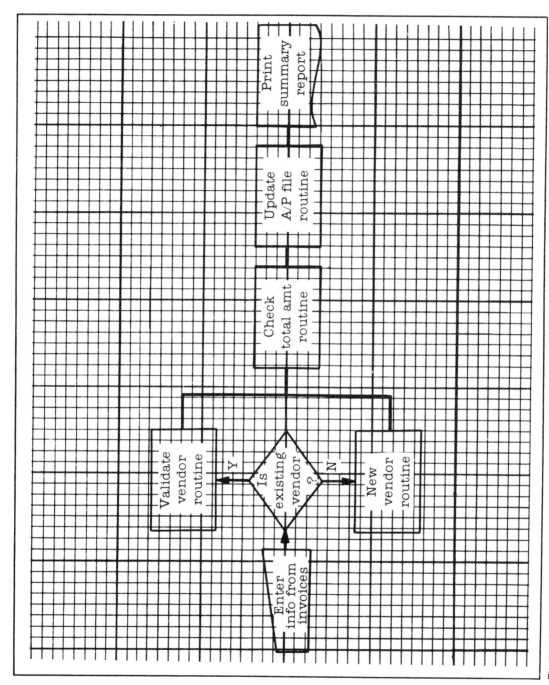

Fig. 2-3. This is a flowchart for the Voucher Entry program. It shows the information that will be entered, the processing steps that take place, and the output that is produced by the program.

```
Pseudocode

Accept Keyboard Entry for Vendor ID
Read Vendor File Until Keyboard Vendor ID = Vendor File
ID or End of File:
If Keyboard ID = Vendor File ID
     then GOTO Good Vendor
If Vendor File ID = End of File
     then PRINT "New Vendor"
          GOTO New Vendor
```

Fig. 2-4. This is an excerpt from the pseudocode that was written for the Voucher Entry program.

signer formulate a complete and detailed program or system design. By identifying the problem in detail, the designer learns what factors must be taken into consideration when developing a programming solution to the problem. The graphic diagrams help the designer quickly visualize the big picture and all the detailed parts that make up that picture. Pseudocode helps the development programmer focus on the specific coding that will be needed to solve the problem.

DOCUMENTATION FOR PROGRAMMERS

Programmers need documentation when they create a new program and when they modify an existing program. If the preliminary design work has been done, your job as a programmer is greatly simplified. (In most cases, if it hasn't been done, you have only yourself to blame!) Working from charts and pseudocode, you can begin writing the code that will put in motion the processing and problem solving you want the computer to do.

Before you write a line of logic code, you should prepare a file description and a variable list for yourself. Include the name of each field, its size, and its characteristics. Figure 2-5 shows a sample file description. Figure 2-6 shows a variable list. These will help you remember which of your "date"

fields holds 6 bytes of packed numeric data and which holds 8 bytes worth of alphanumeric data. Your file description becomes your "cheat sheet" and can keep you from making a lot of mistakes. After all, computers don't like it when you move alphanumeric data into a packed numeric field! It's also important to know what the total size of each input and output file will be.

When you finally begin coding your program, you should include a comment section at the beginning of the code. This section will contain historical information (that's historical, not hysterical!) that can help you whenever you need to review the code or logic of the program. Give your program a meaningful name that describes the problem the program is designed to solve. For example, you might have a CHECK WRITING program in a

```
Invoice File Description

Invoice Date        DA$
Vendor Name         V$
Item Amount         A$
Item Number         N
```

Fig. 2-5. This shows the information that is contained in the Voucher file.

```
Variable List for Invoice Check Program.

DA$    Invoice Date
V$     Vendor Name
A$     Amount of Invoice
M$     Yes/No to Invoice Match
AC$    Yes/No to Amount Checks
```

Fig. 2-6. A variable list identifies the variables that are found within the code for a particular program.

payroll system. Record the creation date for the program. Anytime you make code changes or modifications, you should note the date in this comment section. Your comment section should also include a short narrative that describes why the program was written. You can copy the problem statement if you like. The narrative should also describe how the program solves the problem and mention any special processing subroutines you include.

As mentioned, when you change the code in a program, you should note the date the change was made in the comment section at the beginning of the code. You should also include a brief description of the change. Figure 2-7 shows a comment narrative for a program that's undergone many changes.

In addition to putting a comment narrative at the beginning of your program, you can also include one at the beginning of each major subroutine. The

```
Comment Narrative

REM:   VOUCHER ENTRY
REM:   JOHN KELLEY 1/17/84
REM:   COPYRIGHT JOHN KELLEY 1984
REM:   VOUCHER INFO ENTERED FROM INVOICES
REM:   OUTPUT TO A/P FILE & SUMMARY REPORT.
```

Fig. 2-7. A comment narrative is inserted after the program name and before the first line of code. It briefly describes what the program is designed to do. As changes are made to a program, they are noted in the narrative section.

```
100 REM: VENDOR CHECK RTN
  :
  :
  :
200 REM: DATE CHECK RTN
  :
  :
  :
300 REM: ACCUMULATE LINE AMTS
  :
  :
  :
400 REM: TOTALS COMPARE RTN
  :
  :
  :
500 REM: WRITE MASTER A/P
  :
  :
  :
600 REM: VOUCHER REPORT
```

Fig. 2-8. Experienced coders assign a name to each subroutine. The name gives them a clue as to what the subroutine does in the program. Some programming languages allow you to reference a subroutine by its name as well as the line number where it begins.

subroutine comments can help pinpoint which subroutine is responsible for a particular task. If you don't want to write a detailed comment at the beginning of each subroutine, you can use a comment line to give each subroutine a meaningful name. The name can describe the task for which the subroutine is responsible. The program listing in Fig. 2-8 contains a subroutine with a comment line that names it.

Once the coding is complete, you can print a code listing and use that as a documentation tool. A program listing can provide you with lots of useful information. If a program isn't working, you can review a printed listing to check your code. Many programmers find it easier to work with a hard copy listing because they can write notes, figure calculations, draw arrows, and make other cryptic doodles beside important sections of code.

Printed listings are also used by programmers who are modifying or customizing the code in an existing program. The listing helps them understand the way the program works so they know exactly where to make the changes.

After you've finished with the program, you should keep a printed copy of the code listing on file. If you need to fix a bug or make a change to your program, you can pull out your listing and read it over before diving into the code on the screen. Whenever you change your code significantly, you should replace the listing you keep on file with an up-to-date version. If you change a single line of code, it isn't necessary to reprint an entire listing; just note the change on your file copy. Figure 2-9 shows a program listing that contains handwritten notations.

Programmers need documentation when they are coding. Detailed documentation can help keep a programmer on track so that a program and its subroutines solve the right problems. In addition, this guidance can help a coder develop efficient code that takes into account all aspects of the problem. After a program or subroutine has been coded, a programmer turns to documentation for help in debugging and enhancing the code.

DOCUMENTATION FOR USERS

Program users need documentation as a tool to help them successfully run and understand a program. They want documentation that gives them the instructions, guidance, and reference information they need. In most cases, users don't care about the nitty gritty details about how the code works. All they want to know is what the program can do for them and what they have to do to make it work correctly. Your users will also look for good error documentation. Many users don't understand programming and data processing logic conventions. The mechanics of how programs work are magic to them. When something goes wrong they panic. The problem may be a simple coding error to you, but your user sees it as a major catastrophe.

It's important to remember that your users don't think the way you do (unless they're programmers). What may be obvious to you may be foreign and strange to them. For example, you probably find it second nature to press the enter or return key after completing a command. You know that the computer waits for that signal before trying to see what it needs to do next. That simple act may not be second nature to your user. If you don't tell your user about pressing the enter or return key after each command, he may wait for the computer to do something and think your program doesn't work. While he's waiting for the computer, the computer is actually waiting for him.

When your user makes a mistake, his anxiety level goes up. If you don't tell him how to correct his mistake immediately, his frustration level goes up as he tries a hit-or-miss approach to correcting the error. Simple errors can become stumbling blocks for a new user. New users tend to overlook the obvious when they troubleshoot. Their immediate reaction is usually that the program doesn't work or it has a bug in it. The last thing they think of doing is rechecking the instructions and their typing. You should provide your users with a list of troubleshooting tips that include seemingly obvious suggestions.

Program users tend to fall into two categories: those who read and those who "do." The readers are generally a cautious group. They want to know all about a program before they touch a single key on the computer. The doers, on the other hand, leave the documentation booklet in its wrapper and immediately begin pounding keys in an effort to run the program. The doers will only turn to a reference booklet as a last resort—when they're hopelessly lost and can't figure a way out by themselves. Users

```
10 '              INVOICE CHECK
20 ' J. PELLINO              DEC 1983
30 '
40 DIM A$(256)
50 SCREEN 0,0
60 CLS  HOME
70 PRINT"WHAT IS THE INVOICE DATE";
80 INPUT DA$
90 PRINT: PRINT"WHAT IS THE VENDOR'S NAME";
100 INPUT V$: V$=LEFT$(V$,7): REM 7 char.max
    105 IF V$=" "THEN 90
110 PRINT
120 PRINT"ENTER THE ITEM AMOUNTS"
130 PRINT"ONE AT A TIME.   ENTER ";CHR$(34);"0";
    CHR$(34);" AS AN"
140 PRINT"AMOUNT WHEN DONE."
150 PRINT
160 PRINT V$;" INVOICE, ";DA$
170 PRINT"-------------------------------------"
180 N=N+1
190 PRINT"ITEM #";N;":";
200 INPUT A$(N)
210 IF A$(N)="0" THEN 230
220 GOTO 180
230 REM          TOTAL THE ENTRIES
240 FOR X=1 TO N
250 T=T+VAL(A$(X))
260 NEXT X
270 PRINT
280 PRINT"THESE ITEMS TOTAL TO $";T
290 PRINT
300 PRINT"DOES THIS MATCH THE PRINTED COPY";
310 INPUT M$          AND LEFT$(M$,1)<>"y"
320 IF LEFT$(M$,1)<>"Y" THEN 540
330 PRINT
340 PRINT"EVERYTHING CHECKS OUT..."
350 PRINT
360 PRINT"ONE MOMENT WHILE THE ITEMS AND TOTAL"
370 PRINT"ARE FILED FOR STORAGE."
380 REM          FILE VALUES INTO ".DO"
390 V$=V$+".DO"
```

```
400 OPEN V$ FOR APPEND AS #1
410 PRINT #1,DA$
420 FOR X=1 TO N-1
430 PRINT #1,A$(X)
440 NEXTX
450 PRINT #1,STR$(T)
460 CLOSE #1
470 REM          ALL DONE!.
480 CLS
490 SCREENO,1
500 FOR S=1244 TO 1864 STEP 320 :SOUND S,S/100 :FOR Z=1
TO 10:NEXT Z:NEXT S
510 PRINT:PRINT"INVOICE CHECKING COMPLETE..."
520 PRINT:PRINT"HAVE A NICE DAY."
530 PRINT:PRINT:END
540 REM             VERIFY AND CORRECT
550 PRINT
560 PRINT"LET'S CHECK THE AMOUNTS..."
570 PRINT
580 PRINT"ITEM","AMOUNT"
590 PRINT"-------------------------------------"
600 FOR X=1 TO N-1
610 PRINT X,A$(X)
620 PRINT"OK (Y/N)";
630 INPUT AC$
640 IF LEFT$(AC$,1)<>"Y" THEN GOTO 670
650 NEXT X
660 T=0:FOR X=1 TO N-1:T=T+VAL(A$(X)):NEXTX:GOTO 270
670 PRINT"ENTER CORRECTED VALUE";
680 INPUT A$(X)
690 GOTO 650
```

Handwritten annotations:
- Line 400: (OPEN V$ FOR APPEND AS #1 circled) PRINT CHR$(4);"OPEN";V$: PRINT CHR$(4);"CLOSE";V$ PRINT CHR$(4);"APPEND ";V$
- Line 460: (CLOSE #1) = PRINT CHR$(4);"CLOSE ";V$
- Line 470: REM
- Line 480: HOME
- Line 490: (SCREENO,1) =
- Line 540: REM
- Line 640: AND LEFT$(AC$,1)<>"y"

```
                    SAMPLE RESULTS

   TANDY.DO                              345.67
   12 DECEMBER 1983                      456.78
   123.45                                567.89
   234.56                               1728.35
```

Fig. 2-9. This is an example of an annotated listing for a program being converted from one BASIC to another. Changes that must be made are noted beside appropriate lines.

who read enjoy browsing through well-written reference manuals and entertaining instruction booklets. Users who do will learn how to run a program by hands-on experimentation. The doers want easy-to-find, easy-to-read troubleshooting tips. To be successful, your program documentation must meet the needs of both types of users.

Users Who Learn By Doing

Documentation for users who do should be kept short and to the point. In most cases, instructions displayed on the screen are sufficient. As you write your program, think about what you show on the screen. Do the instructions and error messages you display give the user the information he needs

---

Step-by-step instructions

To create an order for a customer, follow these steps:

1. Choose the Order Entry option from the main menu screen by typing OE in the space provided at the bottom. Press the RETURN key.
2. Type the customer number of the customer for whom you wish to place an order. If this is a new customer, type NEW.
3. The computer will check to be sure you've entered a valid customer number. If you have, you'll proceed to the next screen. If not, a message will be displayed to tell you that the number you typed doesn't exist. Check your typing and correct any errors, or type NEW if the customer hasn't been assigned a number.
4. On the Line Item Entry screen, type the stock number for the item the customer wants to order. This number goes in the first column. Type the quantity being ordered in the second column. The system will automatically display the unit price for the item and the extended amount.
5. After you've finished entering the information for the first item, the system will automatically prompt you to enter another item. If you have more items to include on the order, you can continue to type the stock number and quantity. If you have no more items to enter on the order, type DONE.
6. The system will automatically total the extended amounts for each item and add the appropriate sales tax. When the total amount is displayed, check the figure. If it's correct, press the RETURN key.
7. The Ship To screen will be displayed. The customer's regular shipping address will be displayed. If this is not the address to which the order should be shipped, type the correct address over the displayed address. Be sure to "space out" any unnecessary characters.
8. When all the information is correct, press the RETURN key.
9. The order will be transmitted to the warehouse and a packing list will be printed with the ship-to address you provided.

Fig. 2-10. Step-by-step instructions lead the user through the processing procedures required to run a program.

```
Troubleshooting Tips

     Doing any of the following can cause problems.

 1. Typing the letter O instead of a zero
 2. Typing a zero instead of the letter O
 3. Typing the small letter l instead of the number 1
 4. Typing the number 1 instead of the letter l
 5. Pressing the SHIFT key down when it shouldn't be
 6. Keeping the LOCK key down
 7. Typing CONTROL + character instead of SHIFT + character
 8. Typing SHIFT + character instead of CONTROL + character
 9. Forgetting to press RETURN or ENTER at the end of a line
10. Using the space bar instead of the TAB key
11. Mistyping any characters
12. Failing to turn the printer on properly
13. Typing spaces or special characters where they are not allowed
```

Fig. 2-11. New users tend to overlook the obvious when they try to find their mistakes. Here is a list of some of the common "goofs" new users make.

to successfully run your program. If you're not sure, ask a disinterested person to run through your program and tell you if the messages are helpful or confusing.

Error messages are especially important. If you just tell someone that they've made a mistake, you're not helping them. Most users can figure out for themselves that they've goofed. If you tell your user what the mistake was you give him a clue as to what's wrong, but he still has to figure out what to do next. When you tell your user how to correct a mistake, you ease his anxiety and frustration and the end result is a happy user.

Users who learn by doing will not wade through pages of well-written text. If you include an instruction booklet with your program, one section should include succinct step-by-step instructions on how to run your program. Another section should include abbreviated troubleshooting tips. Figure 2-10 shows an example of some step-by-step

instructions. They hand-hold the user through the operation of the program. Figure 2-11 contains a list of troubleshooting tips. Some may seem very elementary to you, but they probably won't be to your user. Notice that both the step-by-step instructions and the troubleshooting tips are brief and easy to read.

Users Who Read

Members of the second Users' Group either enjoy reading or are too cautious to begin running a program until they know exactly how it's supposed to work and how they can correct any mistakes they make. The same documentation that satisfies the needs of the doers isn't adequate for the readers. Once they're familiar with the program and its operation, the readers may turn to abbreviated instructions and troubleshooting tips as a reference, but initially, they need a longer, more gradual introduction to your progam.

```
Data Dictionary

ITEM  NUMBER
      A unique ID assigned to each inventory item.

ITEM  WEIGHT
      Physical weight of a single stocking unit.

PURCHASE UNIT
      Unit of measure by which the item is purchased.

STOCKING UNIT
      Unit of measure by which the item is stocked.

REORDER
      Indicates whether the item should be included automatically on system-
      generated reorder report.
```

Fig. 2-12. A data dictionary provides the user with program-specific definitions for terms. This excerpt from the data dictionary for an inventory control system shows how definitions are custom tailored to meet the needs of the system. If you looked these words up in a dictionary, the meanings would be different.

The readers look for a detailed narrative that explains why the program was written, the kinds of problems it can solve, and the common pitfalls a user trips into.

Both groups of users will benefit from a data dictionary. This is an alphabetical list of the fields you display on the screen or print on reports. Beside each term, you should provide a definition. The definition isn't the one found in Webster's Dictionary. It describes the way you use the term in your program. For example, Fig. 2-12 shows how the term *bin location* is used in a particular inventory control program.

DOCUMENTATION FOR EVERYONE

As you can see, documentation is used by everyone. It's important for you, as a programmer and designer, to provide the right kind of documentation for each group of users. Each Users' Group has its own interests and needs. You must address and answer those needs when you write your documentation. This is just as important as preparing comprehensive and accurate documentation.

Chapter 3

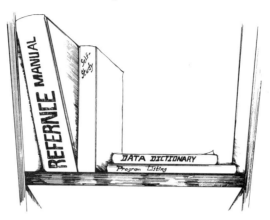

Types of Documentation

This chapter identifies and describes some of the most common forms of documentation you can use. A sample of each type is included along with instructions on how to create documentation using the technique. Appendix A shows how each type of documentation described in this chapter could be used to document the sample program.

CHARTS

Charts are used to show graphically how programs and systems work. Charts can be broad in scope and show the overview of a system that contains many programs. Charts can also show the workings of a single subroutine. A clearly drawn chart can visually summarize many pages of text and can clarify a complex processing procedure.

When you get ready to design or document a program you should consider drawing some kind of chart. This will give you the opportunity to think through the logic of your program while you are designing it by forcing you to layout the processing steps in a meaningful way. After you've written a program, a chart can provide a quick reference as to what the program is doing and how it is doing it.

Charts are useful documentation tools for both designers and maintenance programmers. When a designer thinks through the processing steps required to solve a particular problem, he can use a chart to help him check his logic. If his solution can't be charted using standard techniques, there's a good chance that something is amiss. Maintenance programmers refer to charts to get a sense of how a program solves a problem. While a chart may not tell them which line of code needs to be changed, it can direct them to the task area or subroutine that contains the line.

The most commonly used charts are the block diagram and the flowchart. Another chart type is the Chapin chart. This charting technique can be used in place of a flowchart and is designed to fit neatly on lined paper. These charts are described in detail below.

Block Diagram

The block diagram is used to show high-level relationships between processing modules and tasks. Figure 3-1 shows a block diagram for an accounts payable system. Each of the modules shown in the diagram is made up of many programs, but these programs are not important in a high-level diagram. They would clutter the drawing with unnecessary detail. You could also use a block diagram to show the relationships between the programs in each module.

To draw a block diagram, you will need the following tools: a sharp pencil, graph paper, a ruler or template, and a large eraser. Once you're properly equipped, the drawing is easy.

Before you touch pencil to paper, plan your diagram. You might begin by writing a list of all the things you want to include. This will tell you how many boxes (rectangles) you need to draw. Arrange the items on your list the way you want to appear on the block diagram. This will show you where the boxes will need to be drawn. Your rough layout will also tell you the maximum number of boxes you must draw in a single line. You can draw a block diagram vertically or horizontally on the page.

Find the center of your graph paper. Either you can count the squares across and down, or you can make two light creases. Mark the center point lightly with your pencil. Now look at your rough layout. Find the center of the layout by counting the items across and circling the one that falls halfway between the others, and then doing the same thing for the items running vertically down the page. Circle the middle one. If your block diagram will have multiple rows of boxes, be sure to count from the extreme left to the extreme right, and from the very top to the very bottom; otherwise, your cen-

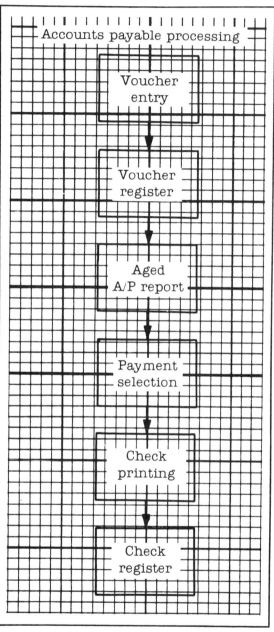

Fig. 3-1. A block diagram provides a graphic overview to a program or system. Each block may represent several programs or modules.

tral point will be inaccurate and you may run out of room.

When you draw your diagram, try to put the vertical and horizontal halfway points as close to the center of your graph paper as you can. Draw your first box at or near the center of the page and then work out towards the edges. Leave at least ½ inch between boxes so you'll have room to draw connecting lines.

Use the lines on the graph paper to help you keep the boxes in a straight line. You should draw the most important line first. (This is usually the one containing the largest number of boxes.) If you're drawing your diagram vertically on the page, be careful when you draw the boxes that branch from the central flow. The second and third branch boxes should line up vertically the same way the central line does. This gives your diagram a neater, more organized look. Your reader will see clearly the various levels within your diagram and won't be distracted by boxes scattered all over the page.

After you've drawn all the boxes, label them. Print your labels neatly with capital letters, or type them.

Draw connecting lines between the boxes and then put arrows on them to show your reader the direction in which to read your diagram.

Put a title at the top of the page. The lettering for your title should be larger than the lettering on the box labels.

Proofread your diagram to be sure you haven't left anything out. If necessary, you can add notes in the blank area near the edges of your page. If a note pertains to a particular section of your diagram, put it near that section. Sometimes it's helpful to draw a dotted line from the note to the section of your diagram it describes.

In most block diagrams, the boxes are all the same size. You can use different sizes of rectangles to show the relative importance of items on your

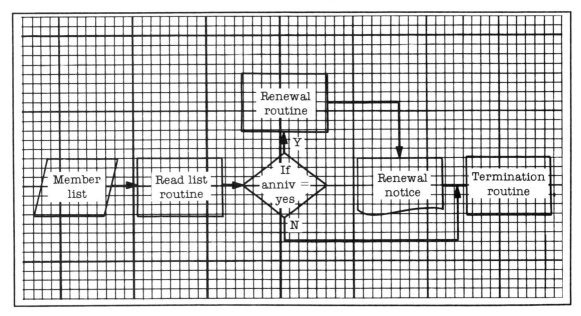

Fig. 3-2. In a high-level flowchart, only the general flow of the logic is depicted. The detailed logic steps that take place at the subroutine level are summarized by the use of processing blocks.

diagram if you like.

Flowcharts

Flowcharts are used to depict the processing logic within a program. They show the sequence of control and the conditions under which it is passed from one module to another. Some flowcharts may show the flow of data through a program rather than the flow of control.

Flowcharts can graphically represent an entire program or the individual tasks and subroutines within a program. If a program is very complex and is made up of several lengthy subroutines, you may want to prepare separate flowcharts for each subroutine in addition to the one you prepare for the program. Figure 3-2 shows a program flowchart in which the subroutines are merely referenced. Figure 3-3 shows the detailed flowchart for a single subroutine.

The technique of using multiple flowcharts helps simplify a complex program into easy-to-follow task areas. It's easier to grasp the overall processing flow of the main program when the subroutines are simply referred to by name. If there's a need to examine the processing in one of the subroutines more closely, the reader can turn to the flowchart for that subroutine and can study it as an isolated element.

To draw a flowchart, you will need the same tools you need for drawing a block diagram. For this

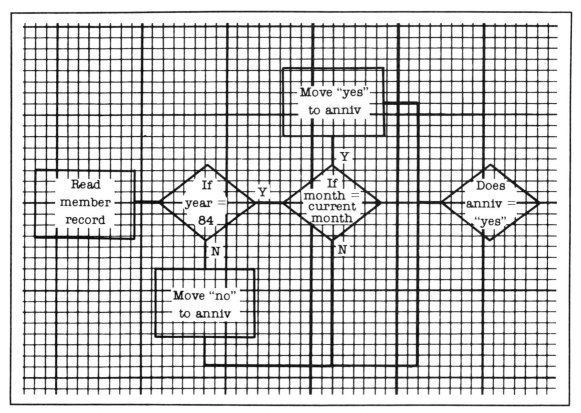

Fig. 3-3. This is a detailed flowchart for a single subroutine. From this flowchart, code can be developed.

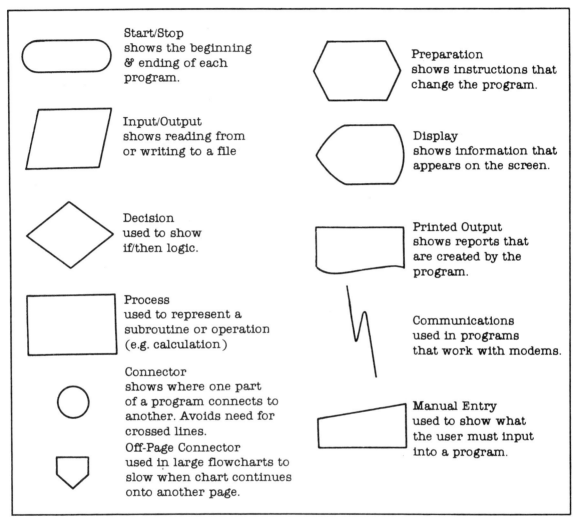

Fig. 3-4. Flowchart symbols have been standardized to promote a common understanding of what they mean. Here are some of the commonly used symbols.

kind of work, a template is a must. A programming or logic template will give you all the symbols you need. It's important to conform to the symbolic conventions of flowcharting. If you do, your reader can always look up any symbols that he doesn't understand. If you make up your own set of symbols, your reader may get lost and won't have any way of decoding your chart. Figure 3-4 shows some of the symbols commonly used in flowcharts.

The central focus of your chart should be the mainline or critical path processing of your program. Special condition processing should be treated as such and should not be mixed in with the mainline. To help your reader zero in on the main processing steps, center them on your graph paper. (You can use either a vertical or horizontal format.)

If your program is very complicated with lots of steps, your flowchart may look very busy. You can eliminate the cluttered look by putting a general flowchart on one page and detailing the subroutine processing on additional pages. Your reader can get an overall understanding of your program from the first chart and then turn to the appropriate page to examine the specific processing for each subroutine.

Look back at Fig. 3-2, which shows a generalized flowchart for a membership renewal program. The list of members is already stored on a file, so the data input symbol was used rather than either the card or manual input symbol. The first processing step in this program is the READ LIST ROUTINE. There may be several steps and decisions that take place within this routine, but they aren't shown on this high-level flowchart. As the list is read, each member's file is checked to see if the member needs to renew his membership. If the member is due to renew, the processing flows into the RENEWAL ROUTINE. If the member is not up for renewal, the processing falls through to the TERMINATION ROUTINE. Notice that the two branches of the decision symbol are marked. In this example, the implications of the decision are fairly obvious. Many times, they are not. This kind of labeling will not only help your readers; it can also help you as you code your program.

Notice that both branches of the decision eventually loop back into the mainline of processing and finish with the TERMINATION ROUTINE. If they didn't the program might be running off into an endless loop after some decision or condition was met.

Figure 3-3 shows a detailed flowchart for the READ LIST ROUTINE in the membership renewal program. The first thing this routine does is to read one of the records from the membership file. The date the individual last renewed his membership is part of the record. That date is divided into two fields. The first is the year of renewal. The second is the month of renewal.

The first decision made in the routine is whether or not the year is equal to "84." If it is less than or greater than "84," control goes to the N branch and the word NO is moved into the ANNIV field. If the year is "84," the Y branch is followed and a YES is moved into the ANNIV field. Regardless of which branch is taken, control proceeds to the next decision symbol where the ANNIV field is examined to see whether it contains a YES or NO. This flowchart is detailed enough for you to use it as a guide for coding.

Before you begin flowcharting, consider your audience. If you're drawing a flowchart for your own benefit as a coding guide or to help you remember how your program works, you may want to prepare a very detailed flowchart for each routine or subroutine. Your fellow users may need the same level of detail if they want to incorporate your problem solving techniques into their own programs. Users who will only run your programs would probably be overwhelmed with very detailed flowcharts. This group would benefit more from the high-level flowchart that shows the overall flow of processing through your program.

Chapin Charts

The Chapin chart is another method of flowcharting the logic and control flow through a program. It uses a vertical format and fits neatly on lined paper. The Chapin chart doesn't use symbols to represent types of information, so you need to include more information in each of its boxes. Figure 3-5 shows an example of a Chapin chart.

Decisions are illustrated by stating the question and then drawing diagonals in the box below the questions. One side shows the Y branch and the other shows the N branch. After a decision is made, the Chapin chart is split into two columns—one for each of the branches. The two column format is

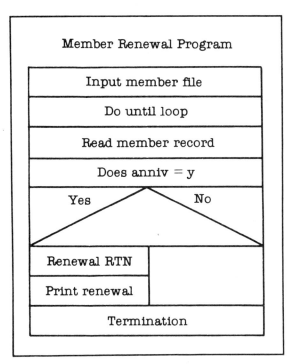

Fig. 3-5. A Chapin chart is a way of graphically representing the flow of logic in a program or subroutine. Its format is well-suited for use on lined paper.

maintained until the two branches meet.

Iterative or repeated statements are charted by putting a box marked DO UNTIL into the chart. The statements, routines, and tasks that are included in the loop are listed in the boxes below this DO UNTIL statement. The end of the loop should be marked with a box marked RETURN. For clarity, you can draw an arrow outside the chart to show the loop more clearly.

PROGRAM SPECIFICATIONS

Program specifications describe what a program must do in order to solve a problem. In a business environment, programmers are given specifications before they begin writing the code for a program. The specifications detail what the pro-

gram is to do and provide the information needed to properly code it.

You can use program specifications when you design and write programs. Your problem statement is equivalent to a specification. It includes a description of the problem as well as a list of things you must consider when coding the program.

While you're writing your code, keep your problem statement (specifications sheet) in an easy-to-see spot. Whenever you're not sure whether or not you're on the right track, reread it. Figure 3-6 shows a sample program specification.

FILE DESCRIPTIONS/VARIABLE LISTS

A file description or variable list identifies the important elements that make up your program. The file description describes the fields in the input and output files for your program. The input file is any information the program needs before it can do its job. The output file is anything that's created as a result of a program doing its job. The variables are the elements that are manipulated by your program during processing.

If you write a program that asks a series of questions, each answer becomes a separate field in the input file. If your program prints a report based on the answers to the questions, then the columns on the report would be parts of the output file.

File descriptions and variable lists can keep you out of trouble. If you list all of the fields or variables and describe how long each one is and what type of characters are allowed, you can refer to your list when you're coding.

There are two types of file descriptions that are helpful. The first is a general description of each field. The description identifies the information you want to appear in the field along with the field length and characteristics. Figure 3-7 shows a sample of this type of field description. The second type of file description may be found within your program. It shows the variable name you've given to each field

Program Specification

This program is designed to create a name and address file that can later be sorted by last name, state, city, and zip code. The file will contain the following fields:

Name 1
Name 2
Initial
Street
City
State
Zip

The Name 1 field can contain 10 letters. Name 2 can contain 15 letters. Initial will contain 1 letter. Street can contain 30 alphanumeric characters. City can contain 25 letters. State can contain 2 letters. Zip can contain 9 alphanumeric characters.

Data for each field is entered separately and ENTER is pressed at the end of each entry. When ENTER is pressed, each field must be validated for appropriate data. If the data is correct, the cursor should automatically TAB to the next field. If the data is invalid, the cursor should return to the first position in the field and the buzzer should sound. If a field is filled with spaces, then the "good data" condition should be used.

Fig. 3-6. This is a sample program specification. It is similar to a problem statement, but it indicates how exception conditions will be handled. A program specification is usually written for the benefit of the programmer who will be writing the code.

and its characteristics. Figure 3-8 shows the same file description as the one shown in Fig. 3-7 as it looks when it is coded.

DATA DICTIONARIES

A data dictionary is an alphabetical list of all the special terms you use in a program. Beside each word, you should explain how that term is used in your program. For example, if you were to write a program to help balance your checkbook, the term *ending balance* might be included in your data dictionary. The definition would describe how your

File Description

Name 1	alphabetic	10
Name 2	alphabetic	15
Initial	alphabetic	1
Street	alphanumeric	30
City	alphabetic	25
State	alphabetic	2
Zip	alphanumeric	9

Fig. 3-7. This is a sample file description. It identifies the various fields contained in the file, and tells how long they are and how each one should look.

```
10  Name-1      Pic x (10).
20  Name-2      Pic x (15).
30  Initial     Pic x.
40  Str-Addr    Pic x (30).
50  City        Pic x (25).
60  State       Pic x (2).
70  Zip-code    Pic x (9).
```

Fig. 3-8. This shows the same file identified in Fig. 3-7, but shows how it looks when coded in COBOL.

program calculates that amount. Figure 3-9 shows a few entries from a typical data dictionary.

SCREEN IMAGES

Sometimes a picture is worth a thousand words. When you prepare documentation, you can include a photograph or line drawing of a sample screen from your program. This shows your users exactly what they will see when they run your program. Figure 3-10 shows a photograph of a program screen. Figure 3-11 shows a line drawing of the same screen. Detailed instructions for photographing screen images are provided in Chapter 6.

To prepare a line drawing of a screen image, you will need a pencil, an eraser, and a ruler or template containing large squares. If you want really professional looking results, you may want to invest in a pad of storyboard paper. This is paper with predrawn screen outlines. They are shaped to look like the screen on your television or monitor. Your local art supply store should be able to provide you with this special paper. If you're going to show picture-like graphics or fancy graphs, you may want to use graph paper.

The key ingredient to screen images is scaling. Use screen outlines that will let you detail the screen to scale. If your screen shows 80 characters

Data Dictionary

CHECK AMOUNT
    The dollar amount for which a check was written.

CHECK NUMBER
    The sequential number that uniquely identifies each of the checks you write.
The number may be preprinted or handwritten.

DATE
    The date you wrote a check (not the date it cleared the bank). The date the bank
posted your deposit (not the date you wrote your deposit).

ENDING BALANCE
    The balance your records show at the end of a period.

RECONCILIATION BALANCE
    The balance the bank shows in your account at the end of a period.

Fig. 3-9. This shows an excerpt from a Data Dictionary that was written to accompany a personal finance system.

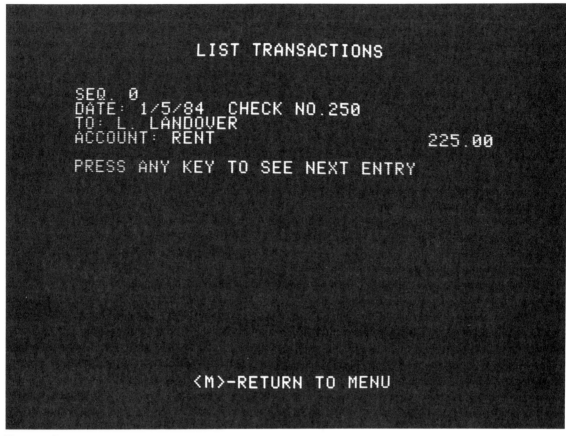

```
                    LIST TRANSACTIONS

     SEQ. 0
     DATE: 1/5/84   CHECK NO.250
     TO: L. LANDOVER
     ACCOUNT: RENT                            225.00

     PRESS ANY KEY TO SEE NEXT ENTRY




                <M>-RETURN TO MENU
```

Fig. 3-10. Screen photos show the user exactly what he will see when running the program. Black-and-white photos usually reproduce more clearly than color photos.

across, you should be able to show 80 characters (evenly spaced) on your screen drawing. If you're showing a picture, count one block for each character you can display.

If you're showing letters, you must be a little more careful. You need to decide how you will do the lettering and then make sure that the screen outline will comfortably hold the maximum number of letters that can be displayed across your screen.

Position the letters and images on your line drawing in the same place that they appear on the actual screen. Otherwise, your reader will be con-

fused and may not recognize the two as being the same.

Some computers offer a shortcut to preparing screen image drawings. They let you print a copy of your screen on paper. If your computer has this feature, you can save time by simply printing the screen and then drawing a screen outline around it.

Work big. The screen images you see in books and documentation manuals may lead you to believe that you need to work with small drawings. In most cases, the original drawings were done large to make it easier on the artist. The large original artwork was then reduced to the size you see in the manual. If you use this technique correctly, the reduced screens will "hide" any slight glitches and wavy lines that may appear on the original. Just be careful not to reduce things too much. If you do, they may be blurred and difficult to read.

PROGRAM LISTS/CODE LISTS

A program list is simply a printout of the lines of code that make up a program. If a program is lengthy, the programmer may print out a partial listing periodically so he can quickly locate the line numbers for the subroutines. Programmers also use code listings to debug their programs. Because the code is printed on paper, the errors can be marked and changes can be written beside the original code. Whenever a program is modified, it is essential for the programmer to review the actual code so that he will know which lines to change and where to insert new code. Whenever you finish a

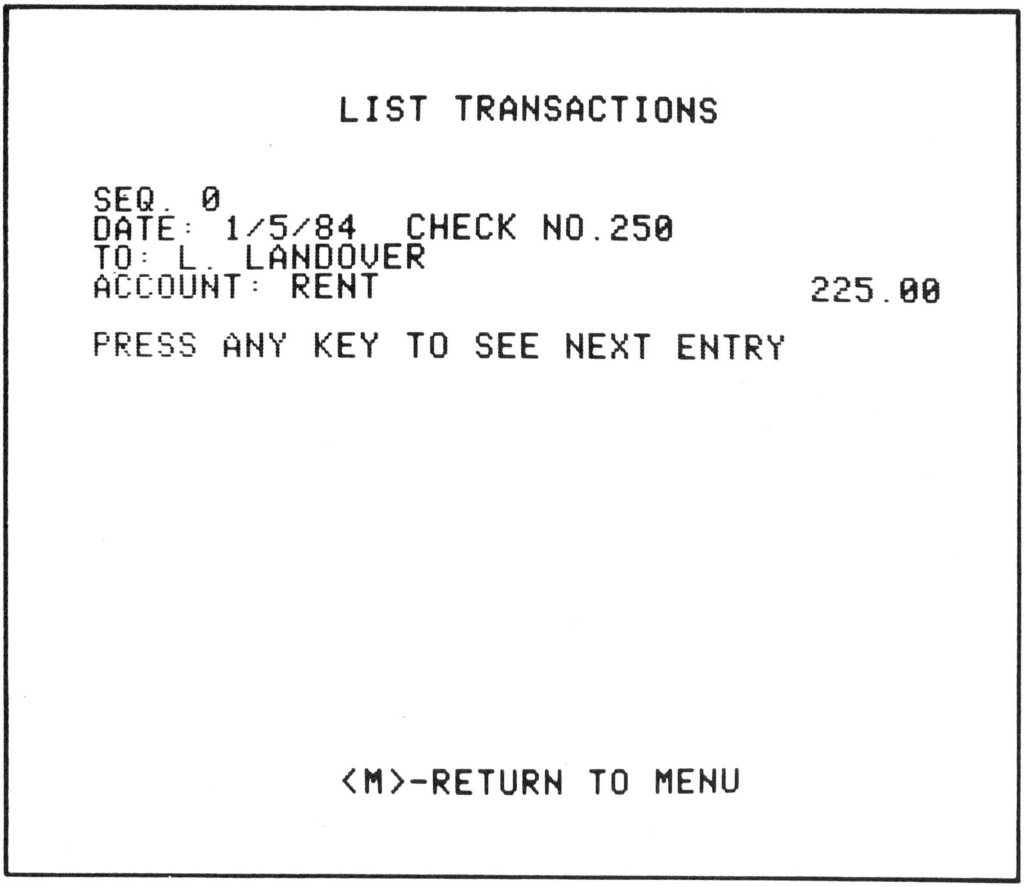

```
            LIST  TRANSACTIONS


      SEQ. 0
      DATE: 1/5/84   CHECK NO.250
      TO: L. LANDOVER
      ACCOUNT: RENT                    225.00

      PRESS ANY KEY TO SEE NEXT ENTRY







            <M>-RETURN TO MENU
```

Fig. 3-11. If you don't have the equipment to photograph a screen, or plan to photocopy your documentation, you may find it easier (and just as effective) to use line drawings to show your screen layouts. This is the same screen shown in Fig. 3-10.

program, you should print a *hard-copy* list of the code and save it for future reference.

You can make your program list more valuable for yourself and others if you make notations on it. There are two ways to do this.

When you are coding, you can embed notes and comments in the actual code as shown in the program in Fig. 3-12. Each programming language has its own special format for doing this. In BASIC, you can use the REM command. In COBOL, you can use an asterisk or exclamation point. Everything on the comment line will be ignored by the computer. Check the manual that goes with your system and programming language to see how to embed comment lines in your programs.

The only disadvantage to using comment lines in the middle of your code is that it can slow down the processing speed of your program. If processing time is critical, you may prefer not to embed comments.

An alternative way of annotating your code is to do it with handwritten notes. This technique will allow you to gain the benefits of having the information without the loss of processing speed.

Regardless of which method you choose to use, the things that need comment-style documen-tation remain the same. Each subroutine should be identified. You can assign meaningful names to your subroutine. The name should briefly describe what the subroutine does. You can expand upon the name with additional comment lines describing how the subroutine works and when it is used. Calculations should have comments associated with them. The comment should describe what the calculation does (for example, calculate average daily balance in a checking account) and when it is used. Your vari-ables should also be identified with comment-names so that you can locate them quickly.

Finally, you should begin each program with a short description. In this description, tell when the program was created, what it was designed to do, when it was last modified, and what the modifica-tions were. If you want to be really efficient, you can even include the number of the lines you changed when you last modified the program.

Special subroutines that you may want to use in other programs can be identified in several ways. You can circle the code, trace over it with a high-lighting pen, or put a bold arrow or asterisk beside it. When you need to find the subroutine at a later date, you won't have to hunt through the entire code listing.

```
]
 1000 REM     display a block of ADAM's memory
 1010 REM
 1020 HOME
 1030 PRINT "DISPLAY A BLOCK OF ADAM's MEMORY"
 1040 PRINT
 1050 PRINT "Enter the starting address of"
 1060 PRINT "the block (in base ten)"
 1065 INPUT "===> "; startaddr
 1070 PRINT
 1080 PRINT "Now, enter the ending address"
 1090 PRINT "of the block (in base ten)"
 1100 INPUT "===> "; lastaddr
 1110 PRINT
```

```
1120 IF startaddr < lastaddr THEN 1160
1130 PRINT "The ending address must come"
1140 PRINT "after the starting address"
1150 PRINT "Please try again..."
1154 PRINT
1156 GOTO 1050
1160 LET baseten = startaddr
1165 PR #1
1170 LET digits = 4
1180 GOSUB 2000
1190 IF error = 0 THEN 1220
1200 PRINT error$
1210 GOTO 1150
1220 PRINT "ADDRESS==> "; hexstring$; TAB(20); startaddr
1230 LET digits = 2
1235 LET loop = 0
1240 LET i = 0
1250 LET place = 2
1260 LET baseten = PEEK(startaddr+i)
1270 GOSUB 2000
1280 PRINT TAB(place); hexstring$;
1290 LET place = place+3
1300 LET i = i+1
1310 IF i < 4 THEN 1260
1320 PRINT TAB(16);
1330 FOR i = 0 TO 3
1332 IF PEEK(startaddr+i) >= 32 THEN 1335
1333 PRINT "* ";
1334 GOTO 1350
1335 IF PEEK(startaddr+i) <= 127 THEN 1340
1336 PRINT "* ";
1337 GOTO 1350
1340 PRINT CHR$(PEEK(startaddr+i)); " ";
1350 NEXT i
1360 LET startaddr = startaddr+4
1365 PRINT " "
1370 LET loop = loop+1
1380 IF loop < 4 THEN 1240
1385 PRINT
1390 IF startaddr <= lastaddr THEN 1160
```

Fig. 3-12. A code list (or program list) is simply a printout of the lines of code for a program.

```
1395 PR #0
1400 GOTO 1040
2000 REM      This subroutine will convert a base ten number
2010 REM      in the range of 0 to 65535 into a hexadecimal
number in the range of 0000 to FFFF
2020 REM      The number will be returned as either 2 or 4
hexadecimal digits.
2025 REM
2030 REM      Variables passed to the routine include:
2040 REM          BASETEN  a base ten number in the indicated
range
2050 REM          DIGITS   a 2 or a 4 to indicate how many
hex digits to return
2055 REM
2060 REM      Variables returned by the routine include:
2070 REM          ERROR    0 for successful conversion or a
specific error code
2080 REM          ERROR$   a message detailing why conversion
was not successful
2090 REM          HEXSTRING$ the converted 2 or 4-digit
hexadecimal value
2100 REM
2110 IF baseten >= 0 THEN 2150
2120 LET error = 1
2130 LET error$ = STR$(baseten)+" is less than zero"+CHR$
(13)+"Can not handle numbers that small"
2140 RETURN
2150 IF baseten <= 65535 THEN 2190
2160 LET error = 2
2170 LET error$ = STR$(baseten)+" is greater than 65536"+
CHR$(13)+"Can not handle numbers that large"
2180 RETURN
2190 IF digits = 2 THEN 2240
2200 IF digits = 4 THEN 2280
2210 LET error = 3
2220 LET error$ = "Can not convert to "+STR$(digits)+" hex
digits"+CHR$(13)+"Can only handle 2 or 4 hex digits"
2230 RETURN
2240 IF baseten <= 255 THEN 2460
2250 LET error = 4
2260 LET error$ = STR$(baseten)+" is too large to convert
```

```
"+CHR$(13)+"to 2 hex digits"
2270 RETURN
2280 REM      convert most significant digit of 4-digit hex
value
2285 LET hexstring$ = ""
2290 LET count = 0
2300 LET temp = baseten
2310 LET temp = temp-4096
2320 IF temp < 0 THEN 2350
2330 LET count = count+1
2340 GOTO 2310
2350 GOSUB 3000
2355 LET hexstring$ = temp$
2360 LET temp = temp+4096
2370 LET count = 0
2380 REM      convert next hex digit
2390 LET temp = temp-256
2400 IF temp < 0 THEN 2430
2410 LET count = count+1
2420 GOTO 2390
2430 GOSUB 3000
2435 LET hexstring$ = hexstring$+temp$
2440 LET temp = temp+256
2450 GOTO 2480
2460 REM      enter here for two-digit hex conversion
2465 LET hexstring$ = ""
2470 LET temp = baseten
2480 LET count = 0
2490 LET temp = temp-16
2500 IF temp < 0 THEN 2530
2510 LET count = count+1
2520 GOTO 2490
2530 GOSUB 3000
2535 LET hexstring$ = hexstring$+temp$
2540 LET temp = temp+16
2545 LET count = temp
2550 REM      handle last hex digit conversion
2560 GOSUB 3000
2565 LET hexstring$ = hexstring$+temp$
2570 LET error = 0
```

Fig. 3-12. Continued.

```
2580 RETURN
3000 REM      This subroutine takes a base ten number in the
3010 REM      range of 0 to 15 and returns a string value
3020 REM      representing that number converted to a hexa
decimal digit
3030 REM      Variables passed to the routine include:
3040 REM          COUNT   a base ten number between 0 and 15
3050 REM
3060 REM      Variables returned by the routine include:
3070 REM          TEMP$   a string representing the hex
value for the number
3080 REM
3085 LET change = count
3090 IF change < 10 THEN   change = 9
3100 ON change-8 GOSUB 3200, 3210, 3220, 3230, 3240, 3250,
3260
3110 RETURN
3200 LET temp$ = RIGHT$(STR$(count), 1)
3205 RETURN
3210 LET temp$ = "A"
3215 RETURN
3220 LET temp$ = "B"
3225 RETURN
3230 LET temp$ = "C"
3235 RETURN
3240 LET temp$ = "D"
3245 RETURN
3250 LET temp$ = "E"
3255 RETURN
3260 LET temp$ = "F"
3265 RETURN
```

Fig. 3-12. Continued.

SELF-STUDY GUIDES

There are many kinds of self-study guides. Some are printed and some are recorded on tapes or records. There are even some that use state-of-the-art videotape and video disc presentations. All are designed to accomplish the same thing. They are a replacement for group classes or one-on-one training sessions. Most major software companies have developed self-study guides for economic reasons. They have found that it costs less to provide this kind of a training manual with a system than to send one of their employees out to train new users.

When you create and market your programs,

you won't be able to go to the home or office of each customer and give individual instruction. Both time and money limitations will hold you back. But you need to be sure your customers get quality instructions on how to use your program. If your customers don't use the program correctly, they may not use it to its fullest potential—or worse yet, they may complain that it doesn't work. A self-study guide can provide your customers with the step-by-step instruction they need to learn to use your program.

A self-study guide is a series of lessons that is designed to teach new users how to run a program. The lessons hand-hold the user and take him from starting the program through using the advanced features. New concepts and operating techniques are presented gradually starting with simple tasks and advancing to more complicated ones. The user can work through the lessons at his own pace so that he masters all the information in one lesson before beginning the next.

The lessons in a self-study guide should be short and cover a limited number of topics. Otherwise, the user will become confused. As the user works through the lessons in sequence, he should be encouraged to use skills and techniques taught in early lessons to solve problems presented in later lessons. The idea is to start by providing a foundation and letting the user build upon that foundation. The foundation consists of the most elementary tasks the user will need to perform to successfully run your program. Once these are mastered, the user can begin to learn ways to deal with more complex problems that require him to combine or resequence tasks. One of the most important things to remember when writing a self-study guide is that you must present ideas in sequence. It's not fair to discuss or mention an option until you've spent some time teaching the option. For example, if you're teaching the user how to add information to a data base, don't mention the points at which he can take shortcuts until you've walked him through the

long way first.

There are many ways to present the material in a self-study guide. You can include step-by-step instructions for each program or program option. When you do this, you need to label the instruction sets carefully and provide an index so that your user can quickly locate the set of instructions he will need to accomplish a particular task. The first time user will probably work through all of your lessons sequentially from beginning to end. The more advanced user will often need to refresh himself on how to perform seldom-used features in your program. By clearly identifying each instruction set, you make it easier for a user to locate the information he needs to deal with a specific situation. Many users will work through the lessons you present until they're comfortable with everyday operations of your program. They won't bother studying the advanced sections. The only time they'll study an advanced operation is when they need to know it.

Another approach to presenting self-study material is to walk the user through each feature of the system. Guides taking this approach are usually full of sample problems. The new user reads about how to use one of the system features and then tests his knowledge by trying to solve the sample problems. To prepare this kind of documentation, you need to explain your program one section at a time. Isolate choices and/or options and treat each one separately. After you have shown your user how to do something, you should provide a test problem so the user has a chance to reinforce what he has just learned. After you've covered several program sections and discussed some features, include a review section with problems that test your user's overall understanding of what's been explained. Force the user to use everything he's learned to solve the problems you present. Always include answers or solutions to the problems you present. Otherwise, your user may be frustrated by not knowing whether or not he came up with the best solution. The answers you provide should include a

A Self-Study Guide

Balancing Your Checkbook

This program is designed to rid you of end-of-month headaches. As you write checks, you enter the numbers and the amounts. When you get your statement back from the bank, you enter the check numbers. The program automatically accounts for the outstanding checks and gives you an adjusted balance you can compare to the balance stated by the bank.

The program is divided into three sections. For now, we'll concentrate on the first two sections.

The first section is Check Entry. This is where you enter the information for checks you write.

Begin by choosing Check Entry from the main menu. Position your cursor under the selection and press ENTER. You can put your cursor anywhere on the line.

The first screen you'll see asks you for the number of your check, the amount, the payee, and comments.

Fig. 3-13. Here are two pages that have been excerpted from a typical self-study guide. The first page is from the beginning of the guide. The second page is from the advanced sections of the guide.

For practice, type the number 1.00 as the check number. (Don't worry, we won't foul up your records. When the pratice session is over, you'll be able to start with a clean slate.)

Special Charges and Adjustments

Now that you know how to keep your checkbook in balance, you're ready to tackle some of the special situations that can throw your numbers into a tizzy.

Special charges are amounts the bank takes out of your account automatically. For example, you may have a check that bounces, so the bank charges you $5 as a penalty. They do this so you'll be more careful next time. Another special charge is for a stop payment. This is when you tell the bank not to cash a check you've written. You might do this because someone lost your original check and you've got to rewrite it (so you don't want both to be cashed if the original suddenly appears), or you might stop payment if you've paid for services (like those of the plumber) and there's a problem (like your sink is still stopped up and the plumber won't come back to see what he missed). Regardless of why you stop payment, the bank will charge you to handle the paperwork and notify the appropriate people not to honor the check.

Because special charges reduce the amount of money in your account, you need to enter them as soon as you know about them. Use the special charges program to do this.

The special charges program lets you enter the date, the amount, and the reason for the charge.

When you enter this information, it automatically and immediately reduces your available balance by the amount of the charge.

For practice, lets enter a charge for a stop payment.

discussion of the solution so the user knows why one solution is better than another. Try to anticipate partially correct and incorrect responses to your problems. Show your user why his answer is wrong, or where a partially correct answer falls short of accomplishing the task. Keep the answers in a special section at the end of your guide. If you put them on the same page as the problem statement, the user will read the answer before thinking up a solution on his own. If you put the answers in the back, the user must shuffle through pages before reading the solution and he's more likely to think about a possible solution before reading the one you suggest.

The format for self-study guides varies greatly. Figure 3-13 shows some pages excerpted from a sample self-study guide. Some guides are full of text while others contain many illustrations. If you're preparing a self-study guide, you should consider including illustrations of some sort. These graphic elements make your guide look friendlier and more inviting to read. It won't look like work. Also, you can frequently explain a complicated procedure more clearly in pictures than you can with text. When you're describing what the user will see on the screen or where to find a special key on the keyboard, insert a drawing or photograph. The graphic element will reassure the user that he's on the right track, and you won't have to waste a lot of unnecessary words describing what a picture can show.

Before you prepare a self-study guide for one of your programs, decide which style will provide your inexperienced users with the best training. Remember, if you prepare your guide correctly, "it's the next best thing to being there."

REFERENCE MANUALS

A reference manual is a tool for the experienced user of a program. It contains brief explanations of how a program works and how to trou-bleshoot errors. Unlike a self-study guide, it does not give step-by-step instructions for running a program. Instead, it concentrates on the problems the program was designed to solve and the tasks the program performs to solve those problems.

Comprehensive reference manuals contain program narratives and system overviews to familiarize the user with the general workings of each program within a system and to show how the various programs relate to one another. Diagrams and flowcharts are usually included to help the experienced user visualize how routines are related and how processing is accomplished. Many reference manuals contain a data dictionary to tell the reader how to interpret the terms that are used in the text. Error code and message listings are provided to expand the usefulness of the troubleshooting tips. These codes and messages help the reader understand the processing condition that triggered the error and the impact that the error will have on both the data and the subsequent processing steps. Figure 3-14 shows the table of contents from a comprehensive reference manual.

REFERENCE MANUAL
Table of Contents

Introduction
System Overview
Installation Instructions
System Check-Out Procedures
Program Descriptions
Program Screens
Sample Reports
Error Codes
Program Flowcharts
Program Listings
Index

Fig. 3-14. A reference manual contains many different kinds of documentation in a single volume. Here is an example of a typical table of contents page from a reference manual.

SAMPLE REPORTS

If your program produces printed output, it's important to show what the printout will look like. The easiest way to do this is to run your program with test information and include the printout with the rest of your documentation. Figure 3-15 shows a sample report from a program.

Meaningful sample reports show more than just format. They show what will happen to different kinds of data. It takes planning to prepare a useful sample report, but both you and your user can benefit from the process. You will benefit be-

Vendor History Report, YTD

Vend #	Vend Name	YTD Paid
1000	Acme Building Supply	$ 578.00
1010	Andrews Printing	$5900.00
1020	******	
1030	Better Office Equipment	$7896.87
1040	Collins Collections	$
1050	Drew Graphics	$ 720.99
1060	*****	
1070	Eagle Photocopy Services	$ 227.86
1080	Fried Accounting	$9288.17

Explanation of Vendor History Report, YTD

This report is traditionally run at the end of a fiscal year, but may be generated at any time. There are three columns of information printed. They are the vendor's A/P number, the vendor name (as it appears on the A/P file), and the total dollar amount the vendor has received in payments.

The dollar amount is always preceded by a $. If no checks have been issued to the vendor, the third column will contain a $ followed by blanks.

Vendors who have been deleted from the A/P file will not be included on this report. The number that was assigned to such vendors will be printed. but the column where the vendor name would appear will contain ******.

Vendors cannot be deleted from the A/P file if any payments have been made since the last annual closing programs were run.

Fig. 3-15. Sample reports show the user what the printed output of a program will look like. A good sample report includes data that reflects many different processing conditions.

cause by trying to show what will happen under different conditions, you will be giving your program a thorough test. Your user will benefit because he will be able to see how different conditions will be handled.

Keep careful notes on the data you input so you can easily connect what goes in with what comes out. You can even include the input information on a separate sheet and include it with your sample report.

You may want to include handwritten notes on the printed report. You can point out unusual situations and describe what caused them.

Accompanying each sample report should be a brief narrative description of the report. In this description, you need to identify all the terms that can appear on your report and define each one. The column headings are probably the most obvious terms that need defining. Don't just repeat the column name as your definition. Tell where the information that appears in the column comes from. If you had to truncate or round the original data to make it fit on the report, be sure to indicate that so your reader won't think the report isn't working correctly. If a column contains figures that have been calculated (e.g., TOTAL BALANCE DUE), describe the calculation as part of your definition for that column name. If the calculated number has been rounded, state the precision.

There may be other information that appears on your report that needs clarification. For example, if you print a string of asterisks to separate information, you should tell your reader that you included the asterisks for this purpose. Otherwise, your user may think they indicate an error condition. If a column contains no information for a particular record, how does it look on the report? If you insert asterisks or dashes, explain that these symbols indicate that there was no date that could be printed.

Your reader needs to understand every word and every mark that appear on your report. Don't

make him guess at anything. The odds are, he'll guess wrong.

If your reports are long and complicated, you should print them on the striped computer paper that is commonly available. The alternating bars of color and white will help your reader follow the report lines across the page. This type of paper also gives your reports a more official look.

PSEUDOCODE

Pseudocode is similar to a program listing except the steps and sentences are written in common English rather than in a programming language. Pseudocode doesn't adhere to the syntax rules that code must. Because it is written in English-like sentences, you can read pseudocode more easily than you can other types of coding statements. In most cases, programmers writing in machine language or other low-level languages use pseudocoding more frequently than programmers writing in BASIC, COBOL, and other high-level languages.

Like flowcharts, pseudocode is often used by programmers before they actually code a program. The program processing steps are written down in the sequence in which they will occur when the program is run. Pseudocode can also help pinpoint sections of code that need to be changed when a program is being modified or enhanced. Figure 3-16 shows a sample of pseudocode.

```
Read Vendor Record
If Vendor-Active Flag = Y
    Then
            Move Vendor No. to Vend-No Print
            Move Vend Name to Vend-Name Print
            Move Accum Pmt Amt to YTD Amt Print
    Else
            Move Vendor No. to Vend-No Print
            Move "******" to Vend-Name Print
            Move " " to YTD Amt Print.
```

Fig. 3-16. Pseudocode lets you work through programming logic without worrying about syntax restrictions. It is especially helpful when programming in machine language.

```
┌──────────────────────────────────────────────────────────────────┐
│                                                                    │
│   Logic List                                                       │
│                                                                    │
│     1. Read the Name and Address File                              │
│     2. Look for Zipcodes beginning with 061                        │
│     3. Arrange the group of records with the appropriate zipcodes in alphabetical │
│        order by last name.                                         │
│     4. Print the list on the screen.                               │
│                                                                    │
└──────────────────────────────────────────────────────────────────┘
```

Fig. 3-17. This is a logic list. It shows the order in which the processing steps should occur.

LOGIC LISTS

A logic list is a short list of the processing steps or subroutines that are used in a program or subroutine. It's more abbreviated than the pseudocode described previously. A sample logic list is depicted in Fig. 3-17.

MULTIPURPOSE DOCUMENTATION

The types of documentation described in this chapter have been uniquely identified to give you a clear understanding of what each is and how it is used. Most documentation is a combination of two or more of the items described. A comprehensive reference manual frequently contains sample reports, flowcharts, and a data dictionary. Self-study guides often include sample reports, which show the trainee what the finished product will look like.

Screen images are included in both development documentation and end-user manuals. File descriptions usually follow program specifications to help the programmer get started with the coding.

Before you write your documentation, make a list of everything that should be included to satisfy the needs of your users. The way in which you combine these items will vary. Sometimes you'll put charts and sample reports into separate sections at the end of your text. Other times you'll want to mix them in with the text.

There is no right or wrong way to combine the various types of documentation. You'll find that the kind of documentation you need depends both on the program and its intended audience. Experiment with different combinations until you're satisfied that your finished product will best meet the needs of your users.

Chapter 4

Getting Started

There are a number of decisions you must make and steps you must take before you actually put pen to paper or fingers to keyboard to write your documentation.

IDENTIFY YOUR AUDIENCE

Before you begin to prepare your documentation, you must determine who will use it and how it will be used. Once you have identified your audience, you can select the most appropriate types of documentation to satisfy the needs of that user group.

Start with Yourself

You are a very important person. You have the ability to solve problems by designing and coding programs and utilities. Don't shortchange yourself by not preparing documentation.

Now, you may argue that if you design and write a program, you obviously know what it does

and how it's designed to work. That is true; but a year from now, you may not remember all the useful details about that program. If you want to borrow code from one program and use it in another, you must first remember which program has the code, and where it's located in the program. If you need to fix bugs or make changes to a program, you need to refresh your memory on how the program "does its stuff" so you don't end up creating new bugs by sticking inappropriate code in the wrong place.

You can save yourself a lot of headaches if you keep a documentation file on every program you write. Even short utility programs deserve a file of their own. In the file, you should keep a copy of the problem statement you wrote to describe the job you wanted the program to do. If you scribbled any flowcharts, pseudocode, logic lists, or file descriptions when you were planning your program, you should put the rough copies in the file. They may not be pretty, but they could save an awful lot of time and trouble if you read them before diving head first into your code to make changes. Finally, you should keep a current code listing in the file. You don't have to print a new listing each time you make a minor change. You can note the change in ink on the listing you already have on file. If you start making major changes, however, you should take the time to print an accurate listing.

If you didn't make any planning sketches or notes, the program listing is a must. Make sure it has a narrative comment section at the beginning so you know what the program was designed to do, when it was written, and what special subroutines it contains.

As a program designer, you'll use your documentation in two different ways. First, you'll use it to locate a particular subroutine so that you can use that code in another program. Second, you'll use it as a reminder of exactly how a program works and what special conditions or limitations are taken into consideration by the code.

Keep all the documentation for a particular program in one place. If your program is short, you can staple the listing together with any flowcharts and notes you have and store the documentation in a clearly marked envelope or file folder. The next time you work on your program, everything you need will be in one place. You won't have to hunt through stacks of paper, cluttered drawers, or notebooks to find what you need. This method also helps keep you from losing important pieces of documentation. If the flowchart is attached to the listing, there's less chance that you'll accidentally throw it out.

Share with Members of Your Users' Group

You may want to share some of the programs and utilities you write with other members of your computer club or Users' Group. When you exchange your programs and utilities with others, you can build a large library of programs inexpensively.

When you study someone else's program code, you have the benefit of seeing how he solved a particular problem. Seeing a variety of coding techniques may also spark ideas for new programs that you could write.

The way in which you share your software creations will vary from group to group. You may supply a copy of your program or utility on a cassette or disk, or you may supply a code listing that must be typed in before the program or utility is operational.

In either case, you should provide the members of your Users' Group with some sort of documentation. The kind of documentation you should supply depends upon how your programs or utilities will be used. If your programs will be simply run for practical or entertainment purposes, then you need to provide adequate instructions to get your users up and running. If your programs are a vehicle to pass around some slick code you've written, then you need to supply detailed information on how the code works and how it can be implemented in other programs.

Profit From a Paying Public

There are so many computers being sold every day that the market for good software programs is expanding at a faster rate then ever before. More than ever, you don't have to be "somebody" to sell one of your programs. If your program 1) solves a problem, 2) provides a faster and more efficient or easier way of doing a specified task, or 3) provides good entertainment, there is probably someone who would happily pay you for the privilege of owning a copy of your program.

When you sell a copy of one of your programs, your responsibilities to your new user are increased. Unlike the members of your Users' Group, you don't know what kind of person is buying your program. It might be a very experienced computer programmer, or it might be someone that just bought his first computer the day before. Because of this, you can't make assumptions.

For example, you can't assume that your user will know how to use the utility you wrote, and you can't assume that your user will understand intuitively the objectives of your game. If you make use of a procedure that is included in the owner's manual that comes with the computer, then you are reasonably safe in assuming that your user could read his manual.

Your documentation, therefore, must be more detailed than it would need to be if you were writing for your Users' Group or yourself. The documentation should be friendly and have an inviting tone, however. There's no need to try and impress your paying customers with a lot of technical terms and long stuffy sentences. Depending on the subject matter, you can even sprinkle some humor in your documentation. One word of caution, however, don't include inside jokes. They may be terribly funny to your friends, members of your computer club, or fellow users, but your customers may miss the humor and feel left out.

If your program is designed to be used as a canned program, your documentation should be directed to the "run only" user. Be sure to include installation instructions that tell the user how to put the program on his system. If any special equipment is required, that should be mentioned up front so the user isn't surprised halfway through the program. Clearly written instructions should not only explain how to run your program under normal conditions, but should also address exception situations. Your text should include lots of examples that show how your program can be used. This will give the user ideas for using the program to solve his special problems.

If your program is designed to be used as a subroutine in other programs, your documentation should be directed to the programmer. It should contain a narrative that explains what the program was designed to do and how it works. Technical flowcharts, file descriptions, and a complete code listing should be included. Any special implementation conditions, restrictions, limitation, or tips should be included so your user avoids surprises when he drops your code into the middle of his program.

Remember your audience. Whether you're writing documentation for yourself or some unknown customer, your documentation must address and satisfy the needs of the user.

CLASSIFY YOUR PROGRAM

Just as the intended audience is an important factor in deciding upon the type of documentation that is needed, so is the type of program you've written. Programs tend to fall into several broad categories. They are business, educational, household applications, scientific, utility, and entertainment.

In part, the kind of audience you attract will be a function of the type of program you write. When you write a utility program that's designed to simplify and expedite computer operations, you're probably going to attract a fairly sophisticated audience of experienced programmers. This group will want to incorporate your utility into their own programs so their programs work more efficiently. If you're writing game programs, you're going to attract people who are interested in enjoying the game play. They won't care how the game works—just as long as it does work.

Let's take a look at the different generic types of programs and the kinds of documentation that seem to work well with each.

Business

Business programs are designed to perform tasks that simplify and expedite daily business operations and activities. The people who purchase this type of program are interested in both running the program and making sure that it is tailored to their special needs. The actual operators of these programs are often nonprogrammers who've been trained in a specific area of the business operation. They may understand the application, but they won't necessarily understand the way the program handles the application.

Your documentation must explain how the program should be run so that it accomplishes the tasks that need to be performed. Good narrative explanations for each program and a generalized system overview can usually handle this. Step-by-step instructions or a self-study guide will help teach the nonprogrammer how to use the computer to obtain the information he needs. Sample report printouts will show the user what information the program can provide, how it's presented, and how to interpret the information. Some level of technical documentation is also required to help the new owner adapt and customize the programs so they meet his specific needs. If you've built in special features that allow the user to control and modify things, then the documentation required to explain how to customize can be in the form of a narrative coupled with some instructions. If the user will need to modify the actual code, you must go into greater technical detail and provide a listing and some flowcharts to help the user understand how the program works and where the changes should be made.

Educational

Educational programs are designed to teach the user something. The documentation that works best with this type of program is a self-study guide. You need to provide the user with a graduated instruction booklet that takes him from an introduction to the subject to advanced topics. The question and answer problem solving format works very well with educational programs.

Your educational documentation will be more appealing if you include lots of graphics. Depending upon the subject being taught, you can use graphics to illustrate a concept, or reinforce what's being shown on the computer screen. If your educational program is designed for young people, then you could even include graphics which both decorate the pages and provide a visual reference as to the topic being covered in a particular section.

Entertainment

The audience for entertainment programs wants to be amused. They're looking for creative ways to pass the time. In most cases, this group wants to simply run and enjoy your program.

The documentation you write must explain what the program does. If it's a game, you need to explain clearly what the objectives of the game are. Your user should have a good understanding of how the winner is determined so he can plan strategies. Screen images can show the user where critical points are in the game so he will recognize them when he gets to them and will know how to play to best advantage.

Game documentation can be lots of fun to prepare. It should be as much fun to read as the game is to play. One way to enhance your game documentation is to pay special attention to the way in which it is presented. Gimmicks can often make the difference between a game that is enjoyed versus one that's highly recommended. Get your user into the spirit of the game from the moment he opens the documentation book. For example, if you're writing a treasure hunt game, you might write the documentation on faded parchment-like paper and stuff it in a bottle. (Don't roll the disk and put that in a bottle, however!) If you're writing a game about combat strategy, you might put a seal across the cover of your documentation and mark it CONFI-DENTIAL. You could also put special hints and strategy tips in code so the user would have fun deciphering the information.

You can let your imagination run wild when you write entertainment documentation. Just don't lose sight of its purpose. You must somehow convey the objectives, rules, and techniques for playing the game amid any extra frills you decide to add.

Household Programs

Household programs are similar to business programs in that they help the consumer perform everyday tasks more efficiently. The main difference is that many consumers will be satisfied with the program in its original form and will adapt their way of doing something to conform to the computer's requirements. Only a few may attempt to modify the program to suit their preferences.

Your documentation should include a general narrative that explains what the program can do and how it does it. You also need to include either step-by-step instructions or a self-study guide so the user can learn the program at whatever pace is comfortable for him. If your program prints reports, you should also include sample printouts so the user will know what to expect, and how to interpret the information.

Scientific

Scientific programs will attract a more sophisticated audience. This audience will probably include some people with programming experience. Depending upon the application, you will need to explain what your program does and how it is designed to handle scientific data. You need to pay special attention to documenting the formulas used in the processing. You might even include a modified data dictionary that includes the formulas used in your program. In most cases, you won't need to provide detailed technical information on the program logic and code, but if your program is designed to become a part of a larger system, you'll need to explain what the user needs to do to incorporate your program.

Utility

A utility program is designed to perform a specific task that relates directly to programming or system operations. Most of the people who are interested in utility programs are programmers. They understand programming logic and they love shortcuts. Your documentation should be technical and complete. You need to explain carefully how the utility should be used and what it does. It's very important to describe both its features and its limitations. If the user can get into serious trouble by misusing your utility, give him lots of warnings and detailed descriptions of the consequences. Your audience will be looking for a brief description of how to run the utility. You can provide this by including a condensed instruction set. If the program is designed to be incorporated in other programs, you need to provide an annotated code listing that shows the user what lines of code need to be reviewed when the utility is dropped into a new program. Because the audience is more programmatically inclined, a flowchart that shows graphically how the utility works would be nice. It would provide the user with a quick reference for the utility's logic.

MAKE YOUR DECISIONS

The first thing your user will see will be your documentation. Before loading your program, he will probably at least scan through whatever material you provide. It's your job to make sure that the documentation you provide is targeted at the right Users' Group and is appropriate for the kind of program you write. To write good documentation that will be read and appreciated by your users, you need to plan. The first step is to identify your intended audience and the type of program.

COLLECT THE INFORMATION YOU NEED

In order to write accurate documentation that's easy to read, you must organize your information. After you have identified your audience and the type of program you've written, you need to collect the reference materials you'll need. Keep everything close at hand while you prepare your documentation.

The things you'll need include a program listing, sample printouts, notes you jotted down while you were coding or testing your program, and any preliminary flowcharts, logic lists, pseudocode, or file descriptions you may have scribbled onto scratch paper.

These are your primary reference tools. From this hodgepodge of information you can develop accurate, usable documentation.

ORGANIZE YOUR MATERIAL

Now that you've decided upon your audience and have collected your primary references, you're ready to begin organizing your material into logical areas.

To help you organize your material and select the documentation that best meets the needs of your intended audience, you should use a worksheet. Figure 4-1 shows a sample worksheet you might use.

The name of the program is listed at the top of the page. The intended audience is identified below it. The rest of the page contains an alphabetical list of the different kinds of documentation you could prepare, to use this worksheet. You can circle or check the items that you feel would provide the best assistance for your audience. By reviewing all of your options each time you get ready to document a program, you're less likely to inadvertently omit something that could be useful to a particular group of users.

DOCUMENTATION OPTIONS WORKSHEET

Program Name:_____

Type of Program:_____

Annotated Listing	Pseudocode
Block Diagram	Reference Manual
Chapin Chart	Sample Reports
Data Dictionary	Screen Images
File Descriptions	Self-Study Guide
Flowchart	Specifications
Logic List	Step-by-step instructions
Problem Statement	Technical Documentation
Program Listing	Test Data
Program Narrative	
Introduction	
Overview	
Installation Instructions	
Checkout Procedure	

Fig. 4-1. A documentation worksheet lists all the kinds of documentation you can prepare. Before you begin writing, circle the items on the list that you'll need to prepare.

GET READY, GET SET, START!

One of the best ways to prepare to write documentation is to prepare a flowchart. If you didn't prepare one before you began coding, going through the mechanics of drawing a chart will force you to check your work and be sure the program processes the way you think it does. The flowchart also becomes a handy reference for you later when you are writing a narrative description of the processing.

Once you've completed your flowchart, you're ready to tackle the narrative. The best way to begin this is to develop a detailed outline. If done correctly, your outline topics become the subheadings in your documentation. The outline details can become the topic sentences in your narrative.

Chapter 5 shows you how to develop a detailed outline that you can use as a basis for writing your documentation.

Chapter 5

Writing Techniques

Writing documentation is not as difficult as it may seem. You don't need to be a technical writer. You don't need to be an English major. All you need is a little organization and some practice. After all, you're not writing a Pulitzer prize-winning novel; you're just trying to give your users a short cut to understanding your program.

As mentioned in Chapter 4, before you begin writing any documentation, you need to study your program and determine who your audience will be. You could be writing for yourself, your Users' Group, or the general public. You need to decide whether you want to keep your program for yourself, share it with others, or make money with it. The decision you make will directly affect the kind of documentation you need to prepare.

Once you identify your audience, you can plan which types of documentation will be most effective. Make yourself a checklist (or use the one in Chapter 4) of the items you plan to include. This will help remind you of your original intentions and prevent you from inadvertently omitting something.

WHERE SHOULD YOU BEGIN?

Begin by writing a problem statement. This is a single sentence that identifies the problem your program solves or the task it performs. If you used program specifications to develop your code, you may be able to extract the problem statement from those specifications.

Tack your program statement up in a conspicuous place. Whenever you start getting off-track, you can reread the sentence. This should help keep all your documentation focused on the real purpose of the program.

Next, as indicated in Chapter 4, gather your resource materials. Collect all the notes, pseudocode, file descriptions, and flowcharts you used as a guide for coding. Take the time to print a current program listing. Compare your resources against your checklist. You may have a headstart on some of the items. With your resource materials and checklist ready, you can begin preparing your look at the program screen. Photograph it if you like, then you'll have a ready reference source that shows you what the user will see and the order in which he must perform the various steps.

IMPORTANT REMINDERS

If you're writing step-by-step instructions, don't rely on your memory. Go to your computer and walk through it to be sure you don't omit something.

Take your time when you're writing your documentation. If you rush through it, you're more likely to make careless mistakes or leave out information that will frustrate your reader. If you become tired or frustrated, leave your work. Come back to it later after you're rested and refreshed. Documentation is, in many ways, like coding. When you reach a point where you just can't figure a way to continue or fix what you've done, it sometimes helps to take a break. When you return, the solution may be very obvious.

Put more information in your documentation than you think your user will need. Remember that your reader doesn't know the program as well as you do. He doesn't know all the features and pitfalls. Things that are obvious to you may be strange and unfamiliar to your user. Users don't generally complain about having too much documentation (except when it doesn't say anything). Most complaints come from users who feel there isn't enough documentation.

THE OMINOUS BLANK PAGE

Most new writers feel that writing narrative text is the most difficult of documentation to prepare. With the best of intentions, they put a clean sheet of paper in front of them and then sit poised with pen in hand (or keyboard under fingers) ready to begin. Almost immediately, the words "This program" appear on the page. And then—nothing. As the seconds tick into minutes, the new writer's anxiety level climbs.

Panic sets in. There's so much that needs to be written, but where should he begin? If he doesn't get started, the documentation will never get finished. A million thoughts spin through the writer's head, but not a letter appears on the page. Writer's Block has found another victim.

Most professional writers are very familiar with this common problem. Because writing is the source of their income, professional writers quickly develop their own individual ways of combatting this annoyance.

Some writers find that pacing helps them overcome writers block. Others switch from writing their documentation on paper to dictating it onto tape. Because it's often the introductory section that causes problems, many writers save that section until the end. They write the most specific sections of documentation first and then tackle the general overviews and introductions. Lots of writers get past writers block by quickly scribbling an opening paragraph and then moving onto more concrete areas. These writers usually return to their first paragraph and completely rewrite it once they've become comfortable with the flow of the text. Brainstorming is another popular technique. Write ten possible opening sentences and then select the one that reads the best.

Each of these methods can and does work. Try them all, and see which works best for you.

Of course, the best trick of all is to avoid getting writer's block in the first place. The easiest way to avoid this is to prepare a detailed outline first and then refer to it when you're ready to write.

HOW TO PREPARE A DETAILED OUTLINE

Once you've collected the reference materials

you need, you're ready to organize them into some sort of logical order. What do you want to tell the user? You might begin by making some general statements about what the program is designed to do or what problem it was designed to solve. Next, you might provide some basic instructions for running the program. Be sure to include information on common mistakes and how to correct them. A third section might cover technical details on the code and how the program works from a programming point-of-view.

Organize your materials into groups based on the section of your documentation that they support. For example, if you prepared a problem statement before designing your program, it would support the first section of your documentation, the section that describes what the program does and what problem it was designed to solve. Flowcharts and pseudocode would support the technical section of your documentation.

After your reference materials have been organized, you're ready to prepare a detailed outline. Figure 5-1 shows a detailed outline. As you can see, the example uses standard outline numbering and indentation.

If you're not used to outlining, you may want to jot a few notes down first and then put them into outline format. Now don't get the idea that you can jot down a few notes and then begin writing your documentation. While there are a few people who can do that successfully, most people need the structure of an outline to put their thoughts in to a descending order of importance.

When you prepare your outline, make it as detailed as possible. The more details you include, the easier it will be to go from the outline to the finished documentation.

Sometimes It Helps to Answer Questions

Take another look at the outline in Fig. 5-1. In this outline, each topic area addresses a specific question. You don't have to copy this technique, but you may find it easier to write a narrative if you ask questions with your subheadings and then answer them with the text. (If you have trouble thinking up questions to answer, try showing your program to someone who has never seen it before. Jot down the questions that person asks.)

AND NOW YOU'RE READY FOR THE ROUGH DRAFT

After you've completed your outline, you're ready to begin writing a narrative description of your program. If you've prepared your outline well, it should be easy to write the narrative. All of the topics associated with the uppercase roman numerals (I, II, III, IV, etc.) become the major sections or chapters in your documentation. The topics associated with capital letters (A, B, C, D, etc.) become major headings within the chapters. Topics associated with arabic numbers (1, 2, 3, 4, etc.) become subheadings and in some cases topic sentences. Lowercase letters (a, b, c, d, etc.) become topic sentences for your important paragraphs. Lowercase roman numerals, (i, ii, iii, iv, etc.) remind you of details you want to include in a particular paragraph.

Figure 5-2 shows how the outline in Fig. 5-1 was converted into a rough draft. Everything's been included. The only problem with this documentation is that it doesn't read smoothly. A little more work is needed to tie the sections together and fix some of the awkward sentences. When that's done, the documentation will be complete.

Proper planning takes the magic and mystique out of writing documentation. If you identify your audience, gather all the reference materials you'll need, prepare a flowchart and a detailed outline, then the actual writing is easy. The only time it's tough to write documentation is if you don't have the materials you need organized into some logical order for presentation. Then you must be a wizard to do all the sorting and organizing needed at the

```
            Detailed Outline
      I.    Overview
            A. What is a job cost system?
            B. How can it benefit your company?
            C. How does it meet your special needs?

      II.   Installation
            A. Preparing the workstation
                 1. Decide where to put the equipment.
                    a. Sketch a floorplan.
                         i.   Lighting and glare
                         ii.  Ventilation
                         iii. Leave room to move around
                 2. Plan space for supplies
                    a. Paper for the printer.
                    b. Invoice forms.
                    c. Statement forms.
                    d. Printer ribbons.
                 3. Don't forget a telephone.
            B. Order forms in advance
                 1. Sample forms
                 2. Suggestions for envelopes.
            C. Plan an installation sechedule
                 1. Get the equipment up and running.
                 2. Read the software documentation
                 3. Train the users
                 4. Test the software
                 5. Parallel testing
```

Fig. 5-1. This is a detailed outline. It gives a writer guidance by helping him organize his material and thoughts into a logical sequence for presentation. It also helps him stay on track while he is writing his narrative text.

same time you're writing the narrative text.

KEEP IT FRIENDLY/MAKE IT INTELLECTUAL

Your rough draft helps you collect your thoughts and decide what to say. The next step is to decide how to say it. Read the sample paragraph in Figs. 5-3 and 5-4. Both say the same thing, just in different ways. Figure 5-3 is very formal and difficult to read. Some people would say it's more intellectual. Figure 5-4, on the other hand, is more casual and easier to read. You might say it's friendlier. Since both paragraphs say the same thing, what makes them different? Lets take a closer look.

Third Person Versus Second Person

Figure 5-3 talks about the user and uses third person pronouns like he and his. This puts a certain

```
            6. Going "live"

    III.  Training
          A. Who needs to learn how to use the system?
          B. What kind of training is provided?
             1. How to introduce new users to the system.
                a. Key users
                b. Self-study guide
                c. Step-by-step instructions
                d. Error codes
          C. What's the most effective way to train new users
             1. Make everyone read the program narrative
             2. Use the self-study guide
                a. Let everyone work at their own pace.
                b. Do all practice exercises.
                c. Encourage experimentation
             3. Print all reports
                a. Keep sample copies as reference
                b. Make notes for future reference
             4. Build data files
                a. Provides repetitious practice
                b. Builds confidence in new users
                c. Gets real work done.
             5. Make documentation available
                a. Keep in easy-to-find place
                b. Encourage new users to look things up
                   i.  Familiarity with text
                   ii. Makes users self-sufficient
```

Fig. 5-1. Continued.

distance between the reader and the text. Who is the user? He seems to be some mythical other person. As you read through the paragraph, you can almost visualize some nondescript fellow carrying out the instructions. But in fact, the user is supposed to be you, the reader of the instructions.

Figure 5-4 talks to you directly. There's no mythical user. As you read through the paragraph, you know the instructions are meant for you. By using the second person pronoun you, the writer immediately gets your attention and gets you involved with the text.

The first paragraph is written in the third person. This is one of the reasons it seems more formal and difficult to read. By putting distance between the reader and the text, this documentation reads like a high-level discussion of how the program works. The reader doesn't get a sense of participa-

TRAINING

Who Needs to Learn How to Use the System?

Anyone who will be working with the system or the information the system provides should be trained how to use the system.

The kinds of training may vary. Supervisors may only need a high level explanation of how the system works while the actual operators will require a working knowledge of how the programs work.

The amount and type of training required will vary depending upon the needs of the individual. Operators need to know how to enter and modify data. Managers need to know how to request and print reports.

What Kind of Training is Provided?

The documentation for the Job Cost system includes a self-study guide, step-by-step instructions for running each program, and extensive instructions concerning troubleshooting and error messages, which are found in the reference manual.

To introduce your staff to the Job Cost system, you need to make some preliminary decisions. First, you should designate one or two key users. You may want your key users to be at a supervisory or management level, or you may want to have one key user be from management and another from your clerical staff.

Your key users should be trained first. They need to feel comfortable with the system so they can provide others with accurate answers to questions. Let your key users read the documentation before anyone else, and give them a chance to experiment with the system and become familiar with the operations.

The key users can then provide training for your other staff members. This training doesn't need to be exhaustive. You just need to be sure the key users show other staff members how to turn on the system and begin running the programs.

Once your operators know how to begin running the programs, let them use the self study guide to learn how to run the programs correctly.

The self-study guide is designed to introduce new users to the system gradually. The lessons begin with easy concepts and procedures and work up to more difficult ones. Each lesson contains several examples or problems that test the user's understanding of the material that's covered in that lesson. At the end of every few lessons, there's a review section that contains questions and problems that test the user's understanding of all the material covered to that point.

Don't rush your users. Encourage them to work at whatever pace is comfortable for them. If you rush your operators, they may finish working with the self-study guide sooner, but they won't have a thorough understanding of the material that's been covered.

Remind your users to repeat a lesson if they can't solve the review problems at the end. If they have trouble solving the problems in the special review sections. tell them to reread the lessons that discuss whatever they don't understand.

After your operators have finished working through the self-study guide. introduce them to the reference manual. Show them where the step-by-step instructions for each program are located and encourage them to use the instructions whenever they can't remember exactly how to run a program.

Show your key users where the error code messages are located in the reference manual. If one of the operators encounters an error condition. the key users should be able to find the appropriate error code and help the operator understand what went wrong and how to correct (or prevent) the mistake.

What's the Most Effective Way to Train New Users?

Make everyone read the program narrative. Most new users have trouble converting from a manual system to an automated system. Tasks that are routine in a manual system suddenly seem strange and difficult in an automated system. Many operators are trained to perform specific tasks in a manual system and don't understand the big picture. Your staff members may not realize that the paperwork they do on a daily basis contributes to a manual job cost system. If they read the program narrative, they'll begin to see how their job and the tasks they perform are part of the system you already have. This will make it easier for them to switch to an automated system.

Use the self-study guide as your primary training tool. The more comfortable your operators become with the documentation booklets, the less they'll depend on your key operators.

Everyone learns at a different pace. Some operators may read through the self-study guide quickly and understand everything. Others may need to spend more time studying the lessons. Don't pressure your operators to rush through the self-study guide. Let them learn at whatever speed is comfortable for them.

Stress the importance of doing all of the problems. It's the only way your operators will be able to check their progress, If they can't do the problems, they won't be able to work with real information. It's better for them to make mistakes on the practice exercises and problems than with your real job cost records.

Fig. 5-2. This is an excerpt from the rough draft that was written from the detailed outline shown in Fig. 5-1. The text needs to be edited, but all the information has been included, and it's in the proper sequence.

> To create a customer record. a customer number is first assigned by the user. This number is entered on the first screen and is followed by the name of the customer. The system checks the existing customer records to insure that the customer number is not duplicated. The user is then permitted to continue with his creation of the rest of the customer record.

Fig. 5-3. This is a sample paragraph written in a very formal style. It uses the third person and the passive voice to achieve it's "stuffy" tone.

tion or a feeling that immediate action is required.

The second paragraph is written in the second person. This is one of the reasons it seems friendlier and easier to read. The second paragraph reads more like a casual chat between the reader and the writer. You'll find that most readers are quickly "drawn in" to documentation written in the second person. They may not be able to tell you why they prefer the document, but subconsciously, they like to feel that the writer is thinking about them. Also, when instructions are addressed to you, there's a greater implication that you're supposed to take action and do what the text tells you to do.

When to Use the Third Person and When to Use the Second Person. From the two examples, you can see that the tone is very different from one to the other. When you write documentation, you should choose the style that best fits the text you're writing.

If you're writing a formal overview of your program, you may feel more comfortable writing in the third person. It will help your narrative seem more authoritative and serious.

If you're writing a self-study guide or step-by-step instructions you'll find that the second person is the better choice. Your user will find your instructions easier to follow and more inviting.

Another consideration when choosing which subject to use is the kind of program you're documenting and the type of users that will be reading your text. If you've written a scientific program, you'll have a different audience than you will if you've written an entertainment program. The scientific user is probably accustomed to reading documentation that's written in the third person and has a formal tone. The game player is more comfortable with friendly documentation that addresses him directly.

There's no absolute right or wrong subject choice for any piece of documentation. The subject you choose is only one element in the overall tone of the writing. Moreover, you must feel comfortable with your documentation. In the end, it's more important for you to communicate information than it is for you to worry about tone and end up not writing anything.

What's Your Preferred Style? If you're like most people, much of the writing you do is in the third

> To create a customer record. you must assign a unique number to each customer. Type the customer number you've chosen on the first screen; then type the name of the customer. The system checks to make sure you haven't duplicated an existing number; then lets you proceed to the next step.

Fig. 5-4. This is the same paragraph as the one in Fig. 5-3. It is written in a casual style. The second person and the active voice are used to achieve a "friendly" tone.

person. School reports, office memos, and most other daily writing tasks use the third person. For this reason, you may feel that you're more comfortable writing in the third person. But before you make a final decision, give the second person style a chance.

Try writing a short set of step-by-step instructions using the second person. To do this, prepare your detailed outline. Next, get yourself a tape recorder. Pretend your detailed outline is notes for a class on how to use your program. Use your notes as a reference and start teaching your imaginary user how to run your program. When you've finished explaining the instructions, stop recording and play the tape back. You'll probably be surprised at the number of times you use the pronoun *you*.

Now put your lesson on paper. (You can skip the "ers" and "ums".) Reread what you've written and fix up any rough spots. You'll be surprised at how friendly and easy to read your step-by-step instructions are. The more you practice using the second person, the easier it will be for you to write your documentation using it. As you master the technique, both you and your user will benefit.

Changing Your Point of View. A word of cau-tion: pick one subject and stick to it. A common problem many new writers share is the tendency to switch subjects in mid paragraph. Figure 5-5 shows an example of this. This paragraph begins with the third person "user" and then switches to the second person "you." This can be both disturbing and confusing to the reader.

The Passive Voice Versus the Active Voice

Another writing element that contributes to the overall tone of the documentation is the voice in which the text is written. Compare the following sentences:

John throws the ball.
The ball is thrown by John.

Both sentences say the same thing, but the second is longer, more complicated, and harder to read. The first is written in the *active* voice. The second is written in the *passive* voice. The active voice is direct and uses a one-word verb structure. The passive voice uses a complex two-word verb structure.

Whenever possible, you should use the active voice. It's easier to read and easier to write. It's like

---

In this program, the customer's purchase order is typed into the system by the user. Each of the items is entered beginning with the item number. The system immediately checks the inventory file to determine whether or not a valid stock number has been entered. If the stock number is correct, the user is permitted to enter the quantity of the item requested by the user. The system then checks to see if a sufficient quantity is on hand to fill the request. If there's enough stock on hand, the system computes the total value of the ordered item. The system multiplies the quantity ordered by the unit price to get that total. You can then enter the next item the customer wants to order. After you've entered all the items, you can add comments and special instructions. Use the COMMENT option to do this. Any comments you add are printed on the picking slip.

Fig. 5-5. This paragraph shows how a writer can switch the tone of text from formal to casual in the middle of a paragraph. Writing that shifts like this is disturbing to a reader and should be avoided.

coding IF statements in a program. You can code your IF statements one after another, or you can nest them. Both ways work. When you code your IF statements one after the other, it's easy to see what's happening in the logic. When you nest your IF statements, you can get confused and cause your program to have errors. When you write in the active voice, it's easy to see what you're trying to say. When you use the passive voice, you can mix up your verbs and cause grammatical errors.

Reread the sample paragraphs in Figs. 5-3 and 5-4. The first uses the passive voice. The second uses the active voice. This is another factor that helps make the first seem more formal and difficult to read. If you decide to use the third person when you write documentation, you can make your work less formal and less difficult to read if you use the active voice.

SENTENCE STRUCTURE

Narrative text is a series of sentences that are put together in a logical sequence to get a message across to the reader. The way in which you structure your sentences is just as important as the words you put in them. Sentence structure is another factor that contributes to the overall tone of your writing.

Documentation that has a formal tone is often filled with long complex sentences. The reader must stop frequently to figure out what the sentences say. Long sentences are also very tiring on the reader because he must pass over a lot of words before coming to a resting place. When a reader must struggle through many long and complicated sentences, his enthusiasm for reading diminishes and he's likely to put the documentation down before finishing it. He's also tempted to scan through the text rather than reading it word for word. This means he may miss important points.

If you write lots of short simple sentences, your documentation will seem choppy. Your reader will have too many resting spots and may get restless. This is just as distracting as lots of long sentences. The best way to write documentation is to combine long sentences with short ones. That doesn't mean you have to alternate long and short sentences one after another. It just means you should include both types in your documentation. Your writing will flow smoothly, but your reader will have the resting spots he needs.

Another element that contributes to good sentence structure is how the sentences begin. Many new writers begin all their sentences with the words *the,* and *this.* While they are two perfectly good words, the reader will get bored reading text in which every sentence begins with one of these words. Try to vary the way you begin your sentences. It's more challenging for you and more interesting for your reader. When you're writing instruction sets, you can use the word *to* to begin sentences. For example, you might say, "To create a customer record. . ." You can also use the word *if* to begin sentences that tell your user about choices he needs to make. When you've finished writing your rough draft, read it carefully to see if you've overworked any sentence starters. If you have, try to rewrite some of the sentences so that they begin with new and different words.

Run-on sentences are an English teacher's nightmare. They're long, confusing, unnecessary, and easily corrected. A sentence should deal with a single idea. When you start putting more than one idea in a single sentence, you're apt to create a run-on sentence. Most run-on sentences use the word *and* to join the ideas together. You can fix a run-on sentence by breaking it up into two or more shorter sentences.

PARAGRAPHS

A paragraph lets you divide your narrative into manageable reading blocks. Each paragraph should discuss a single topic. The topic and idea expressed in the paragraph should be summarized in a single sentence. This key sentence is sometimes called a topic sentence. Your reader should be able to quickly scan through your text and underline the topic sentences for each paragraph. If he then re-reads those sentences, he should get a good idea of what's contained and discussed in your documentation.

Even though a paragraph discusses a single topic, you can sometimes write a lot about that topic. That's okay, but you should try to mix long and short paragraphs in your narrative. When your reader flips through the pages of your documentation, he'll see that the blocks of text are all different sizes. This tells him that while he may have to wade through some long blocks of text, he'll also be able to read through shorter blocks. You may even want to include some paragraphs that are just one sentence in length.

In addition to varying the length of your paragraphs, you can vary the position of your topic sentence. Make it the first sentence in some of your paragraphs, a middle sentence in others, and the last sentence in some. In most cases, you won't have to think about where to put your topic sentence. It will naturally fit in one location or another. If you find, however, that you tend to always put your topic sentence at the beginning of each paragraph, you would try rearranging a few paragraphs to see if you can't relocate the topic sentence. This will make your writing more interesting to read.

GRAMMAR TIPS FOR PROGRAMMERS

This section of the chapter contains suggestions you can use to improve your writing. Don't be alarmed by the headings. This is not an attempt to teach you elementary grammar. You can get all the lessons you need from a book that specializes in that. Rather, this section is tailored to the special writing problem that faces anyone writing program documentation.

Because of the kinds of things that you need to say, and the special terms you need to use, some of the conventions and rules of traditional grammar just don't work. When writing program documentation, you can break the rules of conventional grammar in order to get your point across and keep your documentation technically accurate. The trick is to know when you're straying from traditional standards and to do it for a reason. When you prepare other kinds of writing, like letters and reports, you need to switch back and stick to accepted writing practices.

Subject/Verb Agreement

This is one grammar point that takes no exceptions—for programmers or anyone else. You must make sure that when you have a plural subject in a sentence, you use a plural verb with it. In most cases, this is an easy thing to check for. If you use *and* to join two subjects (for example, Mary and John), then you must use a plural verb. Think of Mary and John as *they* and you won't have any trouble. If you use *or* between two subjects (for example, Mary or John), then you need to use a singular verb. The *or* almost implies two separate sentences. Mary will do something OR John will do it.

Verb Tense

Check the tense of your verbs. In most cases, your documentation would be written in the present tense. If you find yourself slipping into the future tense, change the verb back into the present. For example, if you say, "The computer will print," change it to "The computer prints." In most cases, when you remove the word *will,* you must add an s to the verb. You also need to change any past tense verbs to the present tense. For example, *was* becomes *is.*

When you're in doubt as to whether a verb is correct, try reading the sentence out loud. If it sounds funny, then you may need to make a correction. If you're checking the tense of your verbs, read the entire paragraph out loud. You'll quickly see if you're shifting from past to present or present to future.

Quotation Marks

Because quotation marks are used in coding to surround a literal (something which is to be printed exactly as it appears in the coded statement), you should put punctuation marks outside the last quotation mark. If you put them inside, your user will think that they belong in the code.

Quotation marks are often used to highlight uncommon words or uncommon uses of familiar words. They provide a reader with a signal that a word is unusual or has a special meaning. They also cause the reader to slow down and think about the word. When you write technical programming documentation, you can assume that your reader know many of the special words that you will need to use. In most cases, you can leave out the quotation marks. If you're not sure how knowledgeable your audience will be, put a glossary of terms at the end of your documentation. Less experienced readers can look up the terms they don't know, and it won't slow down your more advanced readers.

Contractions

Most grammar books frown on the use of contractions. They refer to them as colloquial or conversational.

You can use contractions when you write user documentation. They'll give it a more casual tone and help put your reader at ease.

The only time you need to avoid using contractions is when you want your documentation to have a formal tone. Contractions are out of place in formal-sounding documentation.

Be consistent in your use of contractions. If you decide to use them, then use them throughout. Don't use "you're" in one sentence then "you are" in another.

Abbreviations

The rules for abbreviations are very similar to those used in traditional grammar. You can always use common abbreviations like *USA* and *P. O. Box.* States should be abbreviated with the two-character abbreviations standardized by the postal service.

Uncommon abbreviations that may not be universally known by all your readers should be spelled out in full once before abbreviated. For example, not everyone recognizes A/P as Accounts Payable or P/Y as payroll.

When you abbreviate something, be consistent with your abbreviation. If the letters are to be capitalized, use uppercase lettering all the time. Don't switch back and forth (for example, CT and Ct for Connecticut). If you put periods between letters, don't omit them occasionally (for example, U.S. and US). Watch your spacing. If you decide to use P. O. Box, don't get sloppy and write P.O. Box. If your letters are separated by hyphens or slashes, always include them (for example, A/P and AP). Most readers will be able to figure out what you're trying to express, but it's careless and looks like you don't pay attention to details.

Abbreviations can save you a lot of typing, but they can cause problems for your user. Whenever you use an abbreviation, you should spell it out at least once and put the abbreviation in parenthesis after it. From that point on, you can use the abbreviation. This gives your user a fighting chance at finding out what the abbreviation means.

Capital Letters

Capital letters are used in the first word of a sentence and in proper names. Whenever you refer to something that is trademarked or copyrighted, use capital letters in exactly the same way the manufacturer or publisher does (for example, SmartBASIC). The names of programming languages are usually acronyms, so they should be typed in capital letters (for example, BASIC and COBOL).

Coding terms like GOTO and SAVE should always be typed in capital letters, even when they appear as the verb in a sentence. For example, you might say, "If you want to SAVE your program, type the following."

Screen messages should be typed exactly as they will appear to your user. If you wrote your messages in capital letters, type them in capital letters when you quote them in your text. If you mixed capital and small letters, you can do this in your text.

Command keys like RETURN and TAB and CONTROL should be typed in capital letters. In program documentation, words typed in capital letters signal the reader that you are referring to a programming term, command key, or screen message. Therefore, capital letters should not be used to emphasize words in your documentation. Your user will become confused and might think you're showing him a new coding command.

Be consistent in your use of capital letters. If you use a capital letter to show that something is a proper name, you should always use capital letters in the same way. For example, if you decide to capitalize "Trial Balance Report" to show that it is the name of a report, you should always use initial capital letters when you refer to that report.

Capital letters are meant to help the user better understand what's being said. Don't confuse him by inappropriately capitalizing words or using capital letters inconsistently.

VOCABULARY

The words you choose are very important in documentation. They help set the tone, the level of difficulty, and the general clarity of your text.

You'll need to use some special terms when you write documentation. The terms you use will depend on the type of documentation you're writing

and the kind of program you're documenting. When you're describing an accounting program, for example, you'll need to use some accounting terms to explain the tasks that your program performs. This is fine, because your user will probably be familiar with the language that's associated with accounting. The same is true when you write a game about outer space. You can use the special words that apply to that subject. What you need to avoid, however, is using words that are unusual and don't directly apply to the application.

When you're writing a descriptive narrative for your program, a self-study guide, or step-by-step instructions, you should use words that your mother would understand. When you're writing a technical description of how the processing logic works in your program, you can use programming jargon. The difference is the intended audience. Almost anyone might read your "high-level" documentation. The technical documentation will probably attract a more specialized audience.

Be consistent in your use of terms. If you have programmable keys in your program, decide what you want to call them; then stick to that term. Since there are many different terms that are used for this kind of key, you may have a tendency to switch back and forth from one name to another. Your user will have to stop and figure out that programmable keys, program function keys, soft keys, and smart keys all refer to the same set of keys on his keyboard. This is tough on your user and totally unnecessary. Resist the temptation to switch names in mid text. Your user will be able to read through your documentation more easily.

Soothing Words Versus Growling Words

Studies have shown that the words you use contribute to the overall tone of your writing. Soothing words like *pleasure, free,* and *press* have soft, gentle sounds. They can put an anxious user at ease. Growling words like *mistake, tackle,* and *strike* have hard-sounding consonants that can challenge your reader's self confidence.

Text that is written for beginners should be filled with soothing words. Try to use words that have pleasing sounds. In most situations, you can substitute a soft sounding word or two for a rough word. The meaning won't be changed, but the way your reader reacts to what you've said will be improved.

Sometimes advanced users need to be challenged. They can become overconfident and cocky. This usually gets them into trouble. Keep your advanced users out of trouble by using sharper, more challenging words. Text written with words like stop, tackle, and mistake can slow down the advanced user and cause him to pay closer attention to what you're saying.

Most writers and readers don't analyze text. That's a job for grammarians and linguists. It's difficult to pick out the specific words or phrases that make one paragraph friendlier and more encouraging than another. To an inexperienced writer, it may seem like magic; but in fact, all it takes is an awareness of how words can affect your reader. If you're conscious of the effect that words can have on a reader, then you'll be more careful when you write. You'll choose the right words for the right audience.

Problem Words

Certain words can present problems for your readers. Problem words come in several categories. There are words that have double meanings, technical terms, and long words.

Words like *program* have many meanings. In some cases a program is a single subroutine. At other times, the word refers to several related subroutines. It can even be used to refer to a system of related modules such as an Accounts Payable program. Whenever possible, avoid using confusing terms. Replace them with precise words or groups of words that say what you mean.

Another word with many meanings is the word *enter.* If you say "enter the required data" do you mean the user should type in the information or load it in programmatically from somewhere in a stored database? If you say "enter the program," do you mean type the lines of code, boot up a disc, or type RUN? Don't make your user guess at what you mean. Tell him exactly what to do.

Technical terms are often the most precise way of saying something; but this precision is lost when the user doesn't understand the term. If your user has to look up a word in a dictionary before understanding what you're saying, you should be using a different term. For example, a recent documentation manual aimed at new word processor users avoided using the word edit. Even though edit is a commonly used term in data processing, the average newcomer might have to look it up in a dictionary. Words like *change* and *modify* were used.

Long words cause two problems. First, they are usually difficult to understand. Second, they raise the reading level of the documentation. You can usually find a shorter word or two that means the same thing as a long word. For example, you can say letters and numbers instead of *alphanumeric.* You can say "from A to Z" instead of alphabetically. You may have a tendency to write using long words, but they won't impress your user if he doesn't understand them.

Don't Repeat Yourself

One common writing problem is that of overworking "pet" words. If you find that you're using the same word over and over, try to change it. You can use a thesaurus or crossword puzzle dictionary to find synonyms.

HOW TO EMPHASIZE TEXT

There are several ways to tell your reader that

something is important. The method you choose will depend on your preferred style and the limitations of your printer or typewriter.

Type the Text in Capital Letters. Because so many words will be typed in capital letters, this is not the most effective way to emphasize things. If you type a single word in all caps, your reader may think that it is a special term. If you type a sentence in all caps, your reader may think it is a display message he will see.

Change the Type Style You Use. If you have a dot matrix printer or a typewriter with several elements, you can switch to italics or boldface when you type text that should be emphasized.

Underline the Text. This technique will work on virtually any printer or typewriter. If for some reason your printer doesn't underline text (or the command is difficult to issue), you can underline the text after it is printed by using a ruler and pen or pencil.

Separate the Text from Other Documentation by Using Asterisks or Boxes. If you have a special warning note, you can precede it and follow it with a line of asterisks so it will be isolated. If you prefer, you can draw a box around the text after it has been printed.

Use Special Words to Call Attention to Important Points. Technique found in many reference books is the use of words like *attention, warning, note:,* and *hint.* You can center the word above the important text, or you can make it the first part of the text. In either case, once your reader becomes comfortable with your style, he will know what to expect whenever he sees one of the special words.

Another, more subtle, way of stressing the importance of something is to put it into a single sentence and make that sentence into a paragraph by itself.

READABILITY

There are formulas that measure how readable your text is. These formulas take into account the average number of words in a sentence and the number of words that have three or more syllables. Whenever you write, you want to make sure that your reader won't be challenged by the writing itself—what you're saying should be challenging enough! The words you choose should get your point across in the shortest, simplest way possible. Avoid the temptation to show-off your exceptional vocabulary. In most cases you can substitute one or more short words for one long word. If your vocabulary is really good, you shouldn't have any trouble thinking of simple synonyms for difficult words.

Short, simple sentences are the easiest to read; but a paragraph with nothing but short sentences gets very choppy. As mentioned before, mix short, simple sentences with longer more complex sentences. Your text will be more interesting to read, and the short sentences will give your reader a nice break between longer, more difficult sentences.

JUDGMENTS AND OPINIONS

One of the greatest temptations writers face is the desire to tell the reader what he should think. Don't use your documentation as a soap-box from which you can preach your philosophy on life, politics, religion, or the economy. Save your philosophical views for letters to the editor.

A danger in expressing your personal opinions on things is that they may not agree with your reader's feelings on the subject. This can result in an instant turn-off on the part of your reader. He'll think you're a jerk—and how could someone who thinks like that write a decent program?

HUMOR

Contrary to popular belief, documentation doesn't have to be dry and serious. Much of the good program documentation that is currently available is spiced with humor and levity. Humor, used properly, can help keep your reader's attention. It can also reduce anxiety and fear in new users. But documentation is still serious business, so you have to be careful where and how you inject humor into your writing.

Humorous Examples

This is one area where you can lighten the tone of your text. Whenever you supply your reader with specific examples to illustrate how to use your program, make them funny. For example, if you wanted to provide your user with an example of BASIC programming, you might ask him to type the following code:

```
10  PRINT "HELP"
20  PRINT "ME"
30  GOTO 10
```

When your user runs the three line program, the words **HELP ME** will scroll up the screen in a vertical column.

If you provide your user with test data, you can make it humorous. Lets say your program is designed to keep names and mailing addresses in a file. Your test data might include examples like these:

Mr. Humpty Dumpty
10 Wall Street
Great Falls, VA 22326

Mrs. M. Hubbard
22 Cupboard Lane
No Bones, MO 53342

Mr. Peter Pan
18 Flying Circle
Never Never Land, WI 56780

Miss Mary Q. Contrary
78 Garden Avenue
Silver Bells, CA 98778

At first these examples may sound like nonsense to you. But don't worry about them lowering the intellectual appeal of your documentation. You'll find that the majority of users enjoy a little comic relief as they read. Users will also tend to recall humorous examples better than they'll remember more realistic ones.

Humorous Anticipations

Another way to put humor into your documentation is to include it in your instructions. You can do this by anticipating your user's actions and reactions, and then making light of them. This technique will not only improve your writing; it will give your user the reassurance that his reaction (though inappropriate) is perfectly normal.

To illustrate this use of humor, let's say you have a program that does some complicated processing. Your user is asked to enter some data and then must wait a few seconds before the processing is finished. Unless you say something in your documentation, your user may grow impatient and think the program isn't doing anything. If your user is familiar with programming, he may wonder if the program has gone into an endless loop. Here's what your instructions might say:

After entering all the information requested, press the RETURN key. The program will now use the data you supplied to calculate your answer. Be patient! There's a lot of work to be done, so it will probably take a few seconds before you get to see the answer.

This text anticipates the user's reaction to the processing delay and reassures him that everything's working just fine.

You can also use this kind of humor to point out common mistakes and their corrections. For example, if your program asks the user to type the word YES to continue or NO to quit, your user may think it's okay to type a "Y" or an "N". Your instructions might include a troubleshooting tip like this:

> After you type your answer, press the RETURN key. If nothing happens and the computer "beeps" at you, check your answer. (Did you try to take a shortcut and type Y or N instead of typing out the whole word? Shame on you!)

While this kind of humor is not funny in the "ha ha" sense, it still manages to make most users smile. They'll think you're pretty clever to have guessed what they would do wrong. They'll also feel more confident when they read your documentation. After all, if you can anticipate simple goofs, you probably safeguarded your program against major catastrophes.

When to Use Humor

You can inject humor into the narrative overview of one of your programs. It will keep your reader's interest and keep the overview from sounding dry and stuffy. Humor in your narrative will give your users the feeling that you enjoyed writing the overview, and your readers will be more inclined to read the text.

Humorous examples can help you get your point across more quickly and more permanently. Not only will your readers get a chuckle when they first encounter your silly examples, they'll remember them.

Troubleshooting tips that gently tease the user by saying "you didn't by any chance do . . . did you?" will reduce anxiety and frustration by bringing a smile to your user's face. Your user will also have the reassurance of knowing that he is not the first

(and probably won't be the last) to make the mistake.

If you use humor creatively, it can be an effective tool for creating information text that is enjoyable and easy to read.

A few words of caution regarding humor. Sarcasm isn't funny. It makes your reader feel like you're talking down to him. You should also avoid inside jokes. If you belong to a computer club, other club members may understand a reference to an inside joke, but nobody else will. If your reader senses that you're making a joke but doesn't really understand it, he'll feel left out and won't enjoy your documentation.

When NOT to Use Humor

There are some types of documentation in which humor just isn't appropriate. If you try to force humor where it doesn't belong, it will hurt your documentation rather than help it. Here are a few places where you should resist any temptations to use humor.

Charts. When you prepare a chart, you should put meaningful text into the boxes. Notes should be brief and helpful. If you use funny labels, you're likely to confuse your reader.

On-Screen Instructions and Messages. Be very careful of the way you word your displayed instructions and messages. Keep them brief and to the point. Humor tends to turn to sarcasm when it's included in this kind of text.

Psuedocode, Logic Lists, and Code. While your subroutine names may sound funny to a nonprogrammer, they are not the place to use nonsense names. Field names, subroutine names, and program comments are serious and important elements in a program. Don't make them confusing or distracting by injecting humor.

You'll have lots of opportunities to be witty

when you write your documentation. Used appropriately, humor can greatly enhance your writing, but there are times when you need to be serious, times when humor is distracting rather than helpful. Humor is a technique, a tool, a method of getting your point across. It should be included for a reason. Before you write something humorous, ask yourself why you're using humor. If you can come up with a valid reason (like one of the ones described previously), then go ahead, be witty. If not, skip the joke.

OPTIMISM

You're probably wondering what optimism has to do with documentation. Optimism is a very important and powerful tool you can use when preparing your step-by-step instructions as well as other forms of documentation. It gives your reader a feeling of confidence that he can successfully run your program and that the program will work correctly.

There are many ways you can fill your documentation with optimism. You can begin in your introduction by stressing the benefits your program offers its users. Point out the positive features your program offers. Skip over any limitations, drawbacks, or problems. You can cover these later when it's really important for your reader to be aware of them. Don't feel that you're deceiving your user by describing only the positive aspects of your program. Your reader's first concern is what your program CAN do for him, not what it can't do.

When you prepare a self-study guide, take each process individually and walk your reader through the steps slowly. Allow him to build confidence gradually by experiencing feelings of success. Reward your reader verbally for doing things right. Include phrases like,

"That's right!"
"Congratulations"
"You did it"

"Wasn't that easy?"
"Go ahead"

throughout your text. You can even rig your sample programs to display success messages on the screen.

Step-by-step instructions are important to your users. Always present the normal sequence first; then tackle the exception and error conditions.

If you provide a narrative interpretation of a flowchart, stress the normal flow of data. It's important to describe how your program handles exception cases, but your reader's main concern is that they're taken care of. He won't want to dwell on the negative side of your decision blocks.

Your users should feel good about your program and its documentation. If you write with a cynical negative point of view, it will undermine your reader's self-confidence. In extreme cases, you can discourage a user from even attempting to run your program. Neither of you will benefit if this happens.

STEP-BY-STEP INSTRUCTIONS

This documentation technique is very popular for two reasons. First, it lets you tell your user how to do something in logical, easy-to-follow steps. Second, it takes less writing time than the traditional narrative.

This is the easiest kind of documentation to write, and it is the most helpful for the user. If you like absolutes, this kind of writing is for you. Step-by-step instructions are either right or wrong—there's no in between.

How to Write Step-by-Step Instructions

Get a pad of paper and a pencil. Sit down at your computer and get ready to run your program. What's the first thing you need to do? Write that down. Go through your program slowly. Write down everything the user must do and everything he will see on the screen. Be specific! The more details you include, the better your instructions will be. If this seems like a lot of writing, you may want to use a tape recorder and just talk through all the things you do to run your program.

When you're done, type up your instructions so they're legible. Number each step in sequence.

Now you're ready for the field test. Ask someone who doesn't know your program to try and run it using your instructions. Choose someone who doesn't know programming and who doesn't know the application. While your assistant is testing your instructions, keep quiet! Remember, you won't be able to stand next to everyone who tries to run your program from your instructions.

Jot down any questions that come up during the test run. These are the points you need to rewrite so you explain things better. Note any mistakes your assistant makes. If your assistant goofs, then someone else might make the same error.

When the test is over, rewrite your instructions. Clarify anything that caused confusion and add any tips that will keep your user from having problems. After you've rewritten your instructions, find another helper and try the test run again.

It may take several trial runs to perfect your step-by-step instructions. Your second assistant may find problem areas that didn't trouble your first helper. Keep revising your instructions until they are perfect.

The first few times you write step-by-step instructions, you may need to make many revisions. Don't worry. It's better to find all the errors, omissions, and confusing instructions before you release your program and documentation to strangers. You'll also find that after a while, you develop a knack for writing instructions like this. Noticing and recording all the details will become second nature to you. You'll even be able to anticipate trouble areas and guide your users through them.

Step-by-step instructions are very important for your user. Sometimes, they can tend to get lengthy. With experience, you'll find places where you can combine several instructions into a single step. When in doubt, however, split things into separate steps. Figure 5-6 shows an example of step-by-step instructions.

PROGRAM NARRATIVE

The program narrative is the first introduction your user has to your program. It's important to put your best words forward so that your reader is enthusiastic about both your program and your documentation. When your user finishes reading your program narrative, he should have a good idea of what the program is about and what he needs to run the program. There are a lot of things to include in a program narrative.

Begin by giving your reader a short introduction to your program. Explain what the program does, what problems it solves, and how it works. Don't go into a lot of details. There's plenty of time for details later.

Next, you should tell your user what he needs to run the program successfully. Describe the hardware and memory requirements. If your user has a 64K machine, your program may run on it, but as soon as there's a little bit of data built up, the program may not run or may run slowly. It's up to you to be fair and honest with your users. If you need 128K to run your program, say so. This gives your user the opportunity to plan ahead and expand his system.

The next section of the program narrative should describe preliminary steps your user must take in order to run the program. Here you can describe the proper way to load or install your program onto the user's system. If the program runs on a variety of systems, but must be customized depending upon the system, explain this, and tell the user how to handle the changes.

The next section should describe the way in which a user should learn to use your program. If you've included test programs and test data, mention this. If you've written a self study guide or step-by-step instructions, tell your user where to find them. You might also describe any study aids that are included with the package such as charts or data dictionaries.

When your reader finishes reading your narrative, he should have a good overview of what's included in your program and your documentation. He should know what you've provided and what he

---

Step-by-Step Instructions

HOW TO PERFORM DAILY BACKUPS

1. All terminals must be turned off except the one beside the CPU. The printer should be ON and should have paper in it.
2. Mount the tape to be used for the backup. (Follow the diagram inside the door of the tape drive.)
3. Go to the terminal beside the CPU.
4. From the START position, type: I *BACKUP then press the ENTER key.
5. A prompt will be displayed on the screen asking whether you want to BACKUP or RESTORE. Type the word BACKUP then press the ENTER key.
6. A prompt will display asking you to name the tape. The date should be part of your tape name. Here's one way to name your tape; type: MM/DD/YY-BACKUP. Press the ENTER key after you've typed the tape name.
7. A message will display on the screen telling you that BACKUP IS IN PROGRESS. The tape will begin to spin and stop.
8. If you have more data to backup than can fit on a single tape, the tape on the tape drive will rewind automatically when it's full. A prompt will display on the screen asking you to mount another tape.
9. Remove the first tape and mount the next one.
10. When the tape is mounted, go to the terminal beside the CPU and press the ENTER key. You do not need to name the second tape. The system will do it for you.
11. The system will then continue with the BACKUP. The BACKUP IS IN PROGRESS message will be displayed on the screen and the tape will spin and stop.
12. If there is more data to backup than can fit on two tapes, the system will stop at the end of the second tape, and rewind it. A message will be displayed on the screen to tell you to mount the next tape. Repeat steps 8, 9, and 10.
13. When the BACKUP is complete, a message will be displayed on the screen saying BACKUP COMPLETE. The tape will automatically rewind and stop. The printer will then automatically begin printing a list of all the files that were backed up.

Fig. 5-6. This is an example of step-by-step instructions. They are used to walk a reader through the use of a program.

Checklist of things to include in a program narrative

1. A description of what the program does.
2. A high-level explanation of how the program works.
3. A list of problems the program solves.
4. An explanation of the features and benefits of the program.
5. A list of special equipment requirements (e.g. modem).
6. A list of special supply requirements (e.g. preprinted forms).
7. A general description of the program's functions.
8. A statement of program's objectives.
9. Installation instructions.

Fig. 5-7. A program narrative serves many functions and can include many different kinds of information. It's most important function, however, is to give the reader a high level understanding of what the program does and how it works.

must provide. The idea is to eliminate surprises. It's no fun to buy a program and find halfway through running it that you don't have the equipment you need. Most users feel cheated when this happens. They'd rather know up front what's expected from them.

SUMMARY

The techniques presented in this chapter are designed to help you make your documentation text more effective. Good documentation doesn't happen by accident. You create it by deliberately using proven techniques. You decide when to be formal and when to be casual. Humor can be a powerful communication tool when used correctly. Thoroughly tested step-by-step instructions can get your users up and running quickly. A well-written program narrative tells your user what the program can do and puts him in the right frame of mind for reading the rest of your documentation. Positive thoughts keep your user from quitting when he's having trouble understanding what he's supposed to do.

If you use appropriate grammar conventions, make important text stand out, and keep your philosophy and prejudices to yourself, your reader will be able to find the information he needs quickly and without distraction. Pay attention to your writing, and keep it easy to read. It doesn't have to sound like a first grade Dick and Jane text, but the language and sentence structures shouldn't require your user to have a PhD in English.

As you write your documentation, be aware of the techniques you are using. You'll find that your writing will sound more professional and will be as enjoyable to read as it is helpful.

Chapter 6

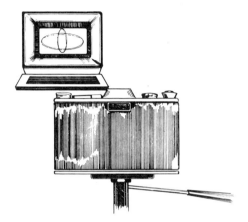

Graphics Techniques

Pages full of text can be intimidating to a reader. They also take a long time to write. You can break up the monotony of solid text by including graphic elements in your documentation. In addition to giving your reader a break from reading the narrative, some graphics can help you shorten your narrative.

Flowcharts can show the relationships between programs or subroutines more clearly and in less space than any narrative you could write. Your reader can scan a flowchart more quickly than he can extract the same information from a few pages of written documentation.

Sample reports and printouts show your user what to expect from the program. Not only do they indicate what information is available, but they show how the information is presented. Some readers will not be able to visualize how a report will look (even with the best narrative description). Users like this need to see either the real thing, or a reasonable facsimile.

Screen images give new users a sense of security. Whether the image is an actual photograph of the screen or just a drawing, the new user can see what the program screen will look like. Many new users are apprehensive about running a new program—so apprehensive, in fact, that they don't take the time to carefully study each screen as it's presented. (It's almost as if they feel there's a time limit on how long the screen will be displayed.) This type of user will quickly scan a screen and then issue a command to continue the program. If something goes wrong, it's difficult to find out why, because the user spent so little time reading the screens that he probably won't remember what was on each one, let alone how he dealt with the information. If you provide screen images in your documentation, you give the user a chance to preview the screens that will be displayed when the program is run. When the user runs the program, he is actually seeing the screens for the second time and is therefore more comfortable with the material and the way in which it is presented. With the comfort level raised and the anxiety level lowered, the user is less likely to make careless mistakes. And, if errors are made, it is easier to track down their causes.

Part of your documentation planning process should be a review of the material you plan to cover with a consideration of whether what you need to say could be better communicated with text or with a graphic element. If you take a few minutes to do this before you begin preparing your documentation, you will not only eliminate unnecessary writing (and save yourself time), but you will be including graphic elements to help better explain something—rather than just for decoration.

CHARTS

Charts provide a neat and organized method for putting a lot of information into a small space. There are several different kinds of charts. Each was developed to convey a particular kind of information. Because of this, you will find that the type of chart you choose for your documentation will depend upon the information you need to depict.

Symbolic Standards

Each type of chart uses a group of symbols that was specially designed for that kind of chart. These symbols are used to graphically represent different things. The groups of symbols have been standardized so that both the chart-makers and the chart-users will have some common ground for understanding the information that is being charted. If this had not been done, two charts containing the same data could look very different. Pity the poor user! Not only would he have to study the chart to figure out what was being said, he would also have to spend extra time translating the symbols every time he looked at a new chart.

For this reason, it is important to learn the symbols that are commonly used for drawing a chart of whatever type you've chosen.

Templates

To help you draw the various symbols correctly, you can purchase templates. A template is simply a shape-guide. It is usually made of flat plastic and contains a variety of die-cut shapes. These shapes correspond to the symbols you would need to complete a particular type of chart.

In addition to helping you accurately draw the various shapes, the templates also help you proportion your charts. Each of the symbols included on a template is scaled to complement the other symbols in the group. If you were left to your own devices, and were drawing a chart in which rectangles were used to hold information, you might make one rectangle twice as big as the one next to it. Your user might wonder if there was any significance to this. Using a template would help you make all your rectangles a uniform size.

When you use a template, you are using a tracing guide. To get the best image from your template, use a sharp pencil. (A mechanical pencil works well too.) Don't use ink. There are two reasons you should avoid this. First, if you make a mistake, it is messy to correct ink lines. Second, when you use ink, you run the risk of getting a blob of ink either on the paper or on the template. If you get extra ink on the paper, your lines will look ragged and unprofessional. If you get ink on the template, you can drag the ink across your page when you move the template. These warnings hold true for all kinds of ink, including felt tip pens.

Figures 6-1 and 6-2 shows two small drawings. The first was done with a pencil. As you can see, the lines are clean. The next one was done with a ball-point pen. Notice how there are extra blobs of ink in the middle of some lines.

If you're concerned that your pencil lines will

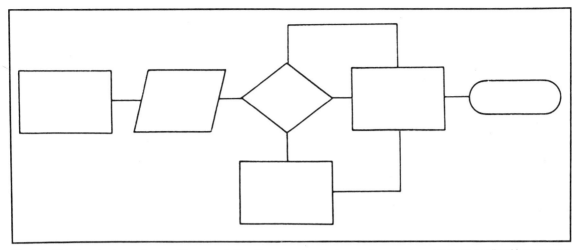

Fig. 6-1. This flowchart was drawn with a pencil. The lines are cleanly drawn. Any smudges clean up easily with an eraser.

be too light to reproduce well, you can always trace over them later using a good quality pen and black ink. Most art supply stores and drafting supply houses carry pens and ink that are specially designed for this type of drawing. The pens come in different sizes so that you can draw lines of different widths. Use a ruler that has an inking edge to draw your lines. This will prevent ink from clinging to the

underside of your ruler and dragging across the paper. If you can't find a special inking ruler at your local store, you can put a few layers of masking tape under any ruler to lift the edge off the page.

Connecting Lines

A chart is made up of symbols connected in some meaningful fashion with straight or curved

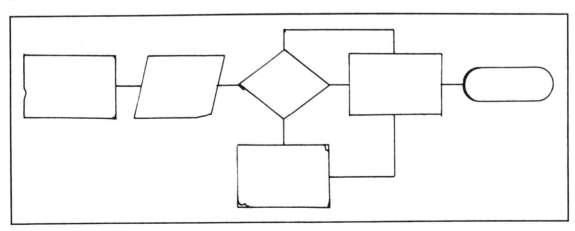

Fig. 6-2. This flowchart was prepared with a ball-point pen. Some of the lines are smudged where the template dragged the ink across the page. The corners have blobs of ink. Several of the drawings have extra lines because the user didn't trace the figures exactly.

lines. Always use either a ruler or a french curve (or protractor) to draw your lines. Even professional illustrators don't draw their lines freehand. If you feel you can't draw straight, even lines you can purchase special tape to do the job. The tape is thin and comes in different line widths. You lay it down on your page where you need to draw a line; then trim off any excess with a razor blade. You can buy this special tape at your local art supply store.

Depending on the kind of chart you are drawing, you will learn the accepted ways of connecting the various parts of your chart. Some charts use arrows to connect things. These arrows can be two sided, open triangles, or filled-in triangles. Other charts use dots to indicate connections. In most cases, a simple line is not enough. It doesn't tell the reader what to read first, second, third, and so on.

Crossed lines are a no-no. You should avoid them whenever possible. Try to plan your charts so that you won't need to have lines cross one another.

It's a Matter of Importance

If you are charting the logical steps of your program, you will quickly see that some elements of your flowchart are more important than others. You may, for example, be able to identify the *critical path* through your program. There may be many side options your user can select, but eventually, he will pass through all the steps in the critical path. (The quickest way to identify this is to read the mainline code for your program. If you've used good coding techniques, your mainline steps will be the critical path.)

Bigger is not better. To show your user which parts of your chart are the most important, you need to find a way to emphasize or highlight them. Don't draw the symbols bigger! You'll get into more trouble than it's worth. For one thing, you will throw off the sizing for the rest of your chart. Besides, there are several better ways to emphasize things.

First, you can use bold lines around the sym-

bols that are most important. Simply trace over the symbols you want to emphasize several times. A similar technique is to put the labels for the important symbols in bolder type or printing. If you're going to have a limited distribution of your chart, you can use color, and either trace over your original lines with a colored pencil or use a light color to shade the entire symbol. If you're going to make many reproductions, you can purchase a stick-on gray tint to lightly shade the inside area of the important symbols. Ask your local art supply store for a 10 or 20 percent transfer screen.

Figure 6-3 shows two of the methods described for emphasizing symbols.

Hierarchy

For this discussion, let's use a typical organization chart. At the top, there is the president of the company. Two vice-presidents report directly to the president. Vice-President A has two supervisors who report to him. Vice-President B has three people reporting to him. Figure 6-4 shows the two common ways this organization chart can be drawn. At the top, the lines of command are drawn diagonally from one central point. In the drawing at the bottom, there are no diagonal lines. The chart at the bottom is easier to read. Because it uses only vertical and horizontal lines, it's easy to keep the various positions in their proper spot in the hierarchy. The horizontal lines reinforce the equality of the two vice-presidents and the five subordinates.

Use the chart at the bottom as a guide when you need to draw a chart showing program hierarchy within a system.

Labeling Your Charts

A chart is meaningless if it isn't accurately and adequately labeled. The symbols you draw will help your reader, but you must label specifically what each symbol represents. For example, it isn't enough to use a report symbol at the bottom of your

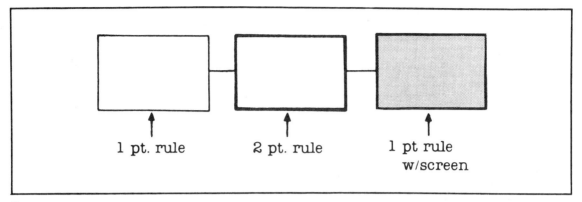

Fig. 6-3. The three boxes in this drawing show how you can emphasize symbols on your charts. The first box is drawn with regular-width lines. The second box has double-width lines. The third box has regular-width lines and a transfer screen with a 20% tint. Don't make your screen tints too dark or you'll have trouble reading the lettering in the boxes.

program flowchart. The fact that the output from your program is a report doesn't tell the reader what kind of report to expect. Be specific. If it's a report showing the checks written during a one-month period, say that.

In addition to labeling your symbols, you may also need to label some of the connecting lines.

Your labels can be typed, printed, or transfer lettered. If you type your labels, take a separate sheet of paper and type all of the labels you need on that sheet. Tape or paste your labels onto your drawing. If you make a typo, you can retype the label. This will prevent your chart from getting caked with layers of correction fluid. Not only is correction fluid messy to work with, but it is also dangerous. If you type on it before it's dry, your letters will be blurred and hard to read. If you have too many layers, or the fluid is too thick, it can crack off and take part of your label with it.

If you print your labels, use pencil. It's easier to erase than pen. If your hand isn't very steady, you can buy lettering guides in a variety of sizes.

Transfer lettering will give your charts a professional look. It takes a few tries to master the knack of getting the letters to transfer correctly and to get them spaced evenly, but it's well worth the

effort. The major drawback to transfer lettering is the cost.

Whichever method you choose, you should always label with capital letters. They're much easier to read.

Where Do You Put the Labels?

Ideally, the symbol labels should go inside the symbols. This is not always possible, especially when you have lengthy names. When this is the case, you can put the name of a symbol outside the symbol. The name should be to the immediate left or right and should be linked to the symbol with a dotted line. Figure 6-5 shows an example of how this type of labeling can be done.

When you label connecting lines, they too should be labeled immediately to the left or right of the line they identify and should be linked with a dotted line. See Fig. 6-5 to see how this is done.

Using dotted lines helps separate the labeling lines from the drawing lines.

If your drawing is very complicated, there may be times when there isn't space to the left or right of whatever you need to label. When this happens, you can pull the label away from the item into more open

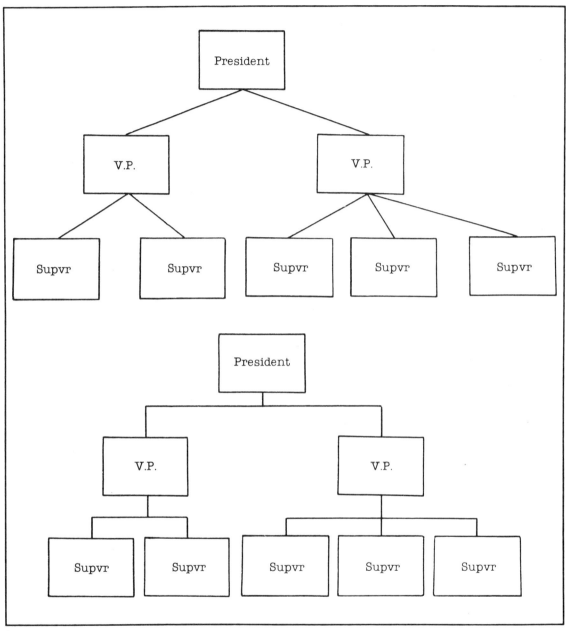

Fig. 6-4. There are two common ways to draw an organization chart. The top drawing shows all of the lines fanned out from a single point. The chart at the bottom shows the second level hanging off a horizontal line. In complex charts, the technique shown at the bottom is easier to follow because boxes at the same level of importance are tied together with horizontal lines.

space by using several dotted lines connected by right angles. Figure 6-5 has an example of this kind of labeling. Though the label isn't as close to the item as you might like, it's still easy for the reader to locate.

Don't use diagonal or curved lines for your labels. If your drawing is too complicated to put your label right next to the symbol or connecting, you need to take steps to keep the overall appearance of the chart neat. Diagonal and curved lines will not only look messy, they will add to the confusion factor of an already busy drawing.

Tips on How to Get a Professional Look

If you are printing your labels or using transfer letters, there are a few simple tips that can help you complete the task easily and obtain professional-looking results.

First, plan your labels before you start. Decide which should go to the left and which to the right. Identify any labels that won't fit inside the symbols they name. A little planning will prevent you from getting part-way through labeling only to find that you put one label in the wrong place and don't have room for another label.

Draw your dotted lines before you begin lettering.

If you're putting a label to the right of something, print your label from left to right. If you're putting a label to the left, work from right to left and spell the label backwards. This can get tricky, so always write the label on a piece of scrap paper so you remember which letters you need to print or transfer when. If you don't do this, you'll look at the label when you've finished and be furious at yourself when you discover that you've omitted a letter somewhere.

Finally, try to keep your lettering all one size. It's easier on your reader's eyes. If the labels are all different sizes, your reader will always be adjusting from one size to another.

How to Plan Your Charts

Have you ever looked through a book that's filled with charts and wondered how the artist managed to get all the charts neatly spaced and centered on the page? Do all of your charts look comfortably spaced at the top or left of the page and then squeezed at the bottom or right side?

If your charts look like you squeezed them onto the page, your reader will have a tough time studying them. You can avoid this problem with a little planning, experience, and graph paper.

Begin by using graph paper with light blue lines. Most photocopiers are "blind" to the light blue. This means that the graph lines won't show up as background on your copies.

To plan the spacing of your chart, you'll need to decide whether you want to put your chart vertically down the page or horizontally across the page. Once you've made that decision, look at the template you plan to use. How many squares on the graph paper does the rectangle use? (You'll usually use more rectangles than any other symbol.) Plan on leaving at least two blank graph paper squares between each symbol. Next, draw a line of rectangles across the page leaving two blank squares between each. How many fit? (If you're preparing a vertical chart, use the same test, but put your rectangles in a line down the page. For vertical charts, you should leave at least three spaces between each rectangle.)

By doing this, you'll know how large your chart can be and still comfortably fit on the page. Next you need to look at what you want to include in your chart. Will everything fit within the maximum limitations of your page? If you've got too many things to include, you have two choices. You can either split your chart into multiple pages, or draw it on a larger sheet of graph paper.

Planning Multi-Page Spreads

If you decide to split your chart into several

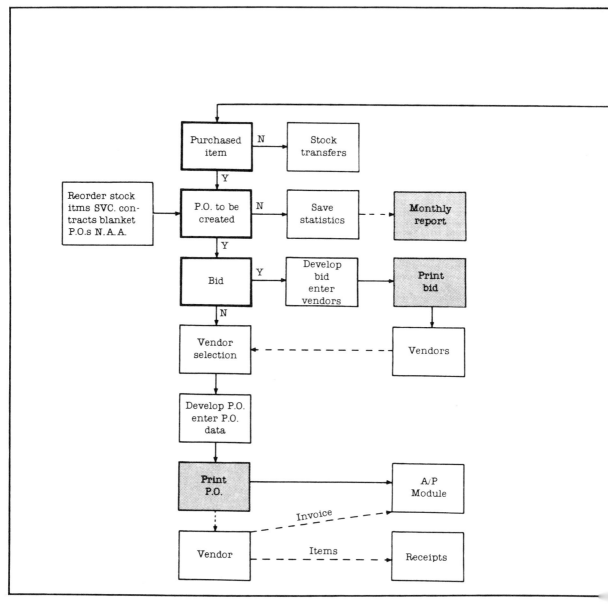

Fig. 6-5. This large flowchart shows the high level processing for a materials management system. The boxes for key processing areas are shown with double weight lines. Printed output is shown with boxes shaded by a 20% screen. Decision paths are shown by small Ys and Ns beside the connecting lines. Activity that takes place outside the primary boundaries of the system is indicated using dotted connecting lines. Warehouse operations are indicated inside the area surrounded by a dotted border. Notice the labeling techniques that are used. (By Barbara Spear for Structured Computer Systems, Inc.)

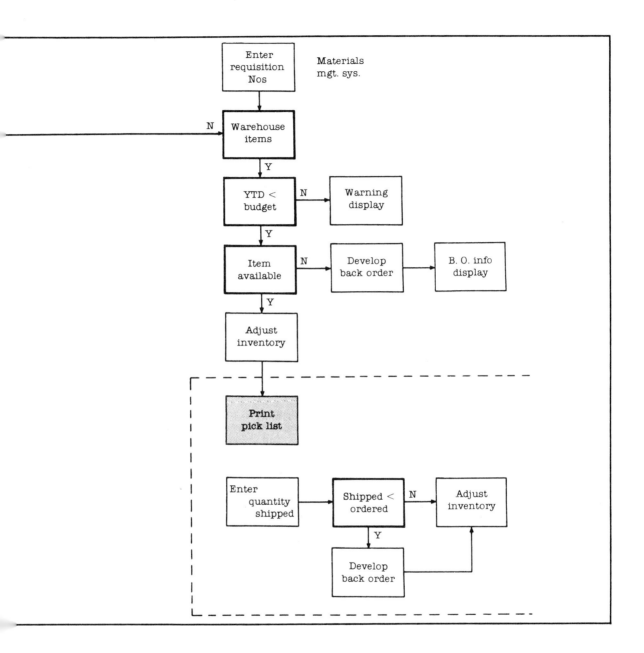

Materials
mgt. sys.

79

parts, decide where you can logically break the chart. This may mean that some pages contain more information than others, but the chart will be easier for your reader to follow. When you split a chart over several pages, check the accepted symbols for the type of chart you're drawing to see what the accepted method for indicating continuance is.

If you draw your chart on larger paper, you may be able to use a copier with reduction capabilities to shrink the chart so it will fit on smaller paper.

With a little practice, you'll be able to neatly space and center your charts on a page. The time you spend planning your charts will be well worth the reward of seeing professional looking results.

Getting Help from the Professionals

Once you've drawn your chart, you have prepared what is called a master drawing. If your master drawing has lots of smudge marks or liquid correction fluid on it, it may not photocopy well. The copier may see shadows and extra lines that you don't see. Also, your original artwork will be pretty fragile. Both of these problems can often be fixed with a little professional help.

A local graphics house or architectual supply company may have a photostat machine. Many printers have these machines as well. The photostat machine (which can be known by many different names) is like a sophisticated copier. It sees only black and white. It won't pick up the shadows that a copier will. If you've used a dotted screen on any part of your work, the photostat machine will capture the look of the screen correctly. It won't show the smudgy image some copiers do.

If you use a photostat machine to copy your work, you can have it reduced to fit on any size of paper. The special cameras that are used are much more flexible than those used in copying machines. All you have to do is say what size paper you want to use.

Another benefit of using professional camera work is that the operator of the photostat machine can center your original drawing on the size paper you choose.

As with any professional work, photostat copies aren't inexpensive; but if you've taken the time to neatly draw a complex chart, it's well worth the investment. The finished product will look really professional. It will photocopy better than your original artwork, and it can be used by a professional printer if need be. Also, the paper that's used for photostats is a lot heavier and more durable than the paper you use for your original artwork.

PHOTOGRAPHS OF SCREEN DISPLAYS

Capturing a screen image on film isn't as difficult as it may at first seem. You can use almost any type of camera for this task. If you have a camera with automatic exposure control you simply point the camera at the screen and press the button. It will probably take a few test shots to determine exactly where to position the camera for best results.

To get a really high quality professional looking photograph, you should use a 35mm camera with through-the-lens metering. If you plan to do a lot of screen image photography, you'll find that a tripod is essential. It will let you take the long exposures that are required without fear of jiggling the camera in the middle of the exposure and blurring the photo.

The standard 50mm lens that often comes on a 35mm camera can be used to take screen photographs, but you'll find that there's less distortion and "warping" around the edges if you use a 135mm or 200mm lens.

To get the best possible image, you'll have to do a little experimentation. Plan to "waste" one roll of film. Take your test roll and follow the suggestions below. Keep careful notes of the exposure time, f/stop, and distance factors you use for each frame. When your roll is developed, you can quickly decide which shots were the best and how to repeat them.

The film you choose should be a good quality black-and-white film. Not only will this produce a clearer image on the photographs, but black-and-white is much better for reproduction. If you really want to use color film, you can, but remember that the shots you get may not be as good as the black-and-white ones and if you decide to mass market your documentation, it will be very expensive to reproduce your work in full color.

Taking the Photographs

When your camera looks at a scene, it averages the light areas with the dark areas until it finds a medium shade of gray. This gray-tone is what is used to tell you where the f/stop should be set.

Your screen probably has black-and-white images. Depending on the kind of display you're using, you have either black characters on a white field, or white characters on a black field. When you take a photograph of the screen, you need to find the average gray value of these characters. Most of the time, the background tone of the screen will be the dominant factor in your camera's averaging calculation. To get a true reading, you need to prepare a test screen that will give you an even balance between the black-and-white areas. You can do this by taking a blank screen and filling it with alternating characters of black-and-white. If possible, you should create a checkerboard effect by using blocks of light and dark. If you don't have a key that will produce a block on the screen, use a very condensed letter like capital W. Leave a blank space between characters to allow the background tone of the screen to display. Take a light measurement against this test screen and you'll have the true medium gray reading for your system.

When you take your readings and your photographs, make sure you're working in a darkened room with no artificial lighting. Room lights and daylight can produce reflected images on your screen which will distort your photograph.

Set your camera on a tripod and position it so that you fill the frame with the screen image. This will prevent your camera from getting faulty readings from surrounding objects, including the casing of your monitor or television.

The length of your exposure should be no less than 1/30 second. If possible, use an even longer setting. The reason for doing this is that a screen refreshes itself periodically and if your exposure time is too short, you may actually lose part of the screen on the photo.

If you're serious about photographing your screen images, you should take the time to experiment with your camera. With a little practice, you can get professional looking photos every time. Just remember, if you're using a through-the-lens metering system, what you see is what you'll get. If something doesn't look quite right, try to figure out what the problem is and correct it.

Figures 6-6 through 6-9 show samples of screen shots taken using the equipment and methods described in this chapter.

CARTOONS AND ILLUSTRATIONS

Cartoons and drawings can be valuable assets to your documentation if they are used properly. They provide a visual break for your reader. Cartoons can add comic relief to a serious instruction manual. They can also graphically reinforce or summarize what you've said in the text. Cartoons and illustrations should always be included as an enhancement to your text; they should not be used merely as decoration or distract from your text.

Cartoons

A cartoon is a humorous illustration. Cartoons are used to add humor to your documentation. You can create a cartoon that humorously summarizes the ideas contained within an entire chapter or sec-

Fig. 6-6. Here is a screen shot showing a graphic.

tion of your documentation, or you can use a cartoon to illustrate a single point.

Cartooning is a graphic technique in the same way that the use of the second person (you) is a writing technique. If you decide to incorporate cartooning into your documentation, you need to be consistent in its use. Don't just drop a single cartoon into the middle of your text. No matter how relevant the cartoon is to the particular section of text, it will become a distraction to your reader. Instead, you should plan to include cartoons throughout your documentation.

In addition to supporting specific parts of your text, your cartoons should relate to one another. If your reader decides to look through your docu-

mentation and study your cartoons, he should be able to see a pattern developing.

There are many ways to pattern your cartoons. First, you can establish a format and use that for each cartoon you draw. For example, you might decide to create a character and feature that character in all your cartoons. The character you create may be realistic or whimsical.

Another way to give continuity to your cartoons is to choose a format and stick with it. You can put a border line around your cartoons, or let them "float" on the page. It doesn't matter which format you choose—as long as you're consistent. Captions are a second format consideration. You may want to include captions with each cartoon, or you may decide to omit them. Again, it doesn't really matter as long as you're consistent.

Many times, "floating" cartoons appear at the beginning of each chapter or section of a documentation manual. They humorously depict the topics discussed in the text. In a sense, they give the reader a preview of what will be covered by the narrative.

Cartoons are particularly effective and appropriate in users manuals where the tone of the text is casual and friendly. The mere presence of cartoons suggest to readers that the manual will be easy and enjoyable to read. Some sample cartoons are shown in Fig. 6-10.

Instructive Illustrations

Sometimes an illustration can be used to graphically show the reader what the text is saying. This kind of drawing helps the user understand exactly what you want him to do.

For example, if you are writing step-by-step instructions, you might include a line drawing of the key you want your user to press as shown in Fig. 6-11. The reader can then find the key on his

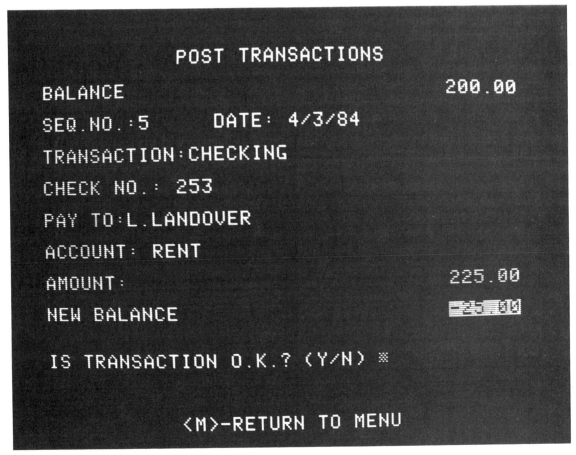

Fig. 6-7. Here is a screen shot showing an entry screen.

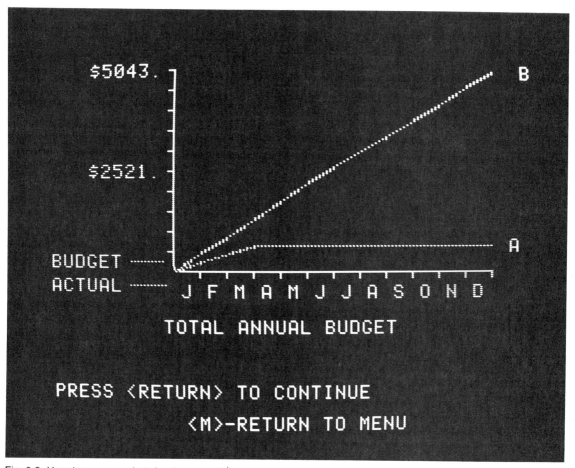

Fig. 6-8. Here is a screen shot showing a graph.

keyboard that looks like the one in your drawing. There's no question in his mind as to which key you mean.

An instructive illustration should be accurately drawn. You don't have the same whimsical leeway you do when you're drawing cartoons.

The instructive drawing supports and further explains a very specific section of text. For this reason, it should be positioned right after the text it illustrates. When you type your documentation, remember to leave extra space in those places

where you plan to include drawings.

General Illustrations

A general illustration is like a cartoon except that it doesn't have to be humorous. You can use many different kinds of drawings to give your reader a visual break from the text. Your drawings should have a similar theme and should enhance your documentation text. You might want to include an illustration at the beginning of each chapter or section. Here are some suggestions for the kinds of illustrations you might use to enhance your documentation.

Technical Documentation. At the beginning of your documentation, include a high-level flowchart depicting the entire program or system. At the beginning of each section, show a detailed flowchart depicting the information discussed in the section, as shown in Fig. 6-12.

User Manual for a Menu-Driven Program. At the beginning of your documentation, show a line drawing of the master menu for your program as shown in Fig. 6-13. As you describe each section, repeat the master menu screen, but underline or use boldface type on the selection you're describing.

User Manual for a Multi-Program System. If you've written a personal finance system, you might include a drawing at the beginning of each section to illustrate the program the section describes. For example, you might draw a fictitious bank statement to illustrate the check reconciliation program.

Technical Manual for a Utility Programs. At the beginning of the documentation for each utility, you might graphically depict what the utility can do for the user. For example, if you've written a utility

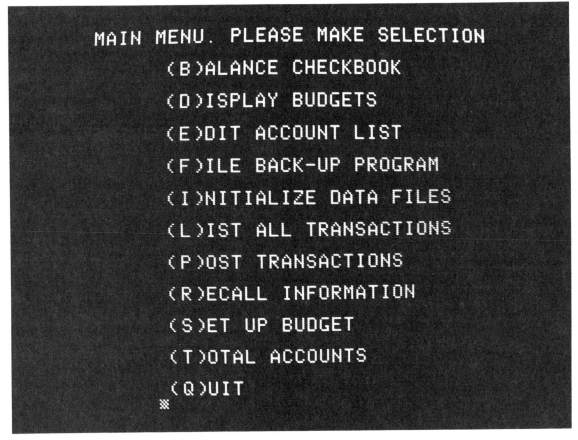

Fig. 6-9. Here is a screen shot showing a program menu.

85

Keeping track of repairs

Fig. 6-10. Here are several cartoon techniques. All are different ways of illustrating the same program.

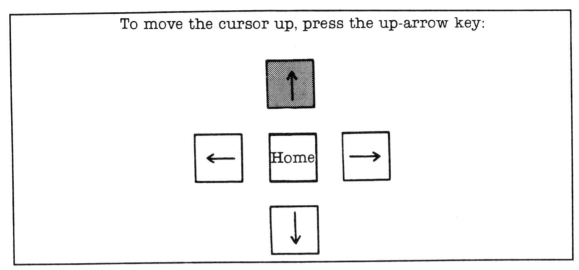

Fig. 6-11. Instructional illustrations should be accurate and easy to read. They should be placed immediately after the text they clarify. In this drawing, the up-arrow was shaded with a 20% screen to distinguish it from the other cursor control keys.

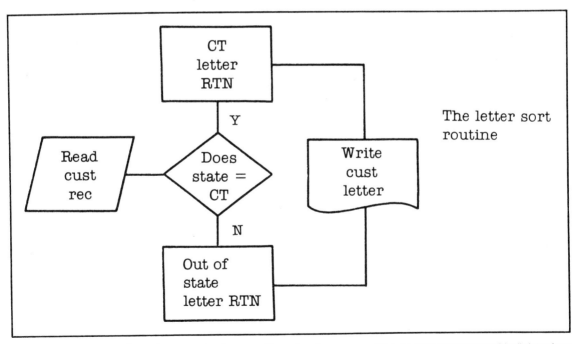

Fig. 6-12. This flowchart shows the processing for a specific routine. You can use this type of flowchart to graphically introduce new topics in your technical documentation.

that sorts information, you could show someone putting sheets of paper into bins. The labels on the bins would correspond to the information your utility sorts.

User Manual for a Game. At the beginning of your manual, you might include an illustration that captures the flavor of your game. As you describe how the game is played, you might pull out sections of your overview drawing. For example, if you've written an adventure game in which the superhero must fight a series of enemies in order to win, you might show all the villians in your overview drawing and then show individual enemies throughout your instruction booklet.

Essential Concepts
Concerning Cartoons and Illustrations

Cartoons and illustrations are effective documentation tools when used appropriately. They can support and enhance your text. Not only do they provide your reader with a visual break from the narrative, they also reinforce what you're saying. When the user goes to run your program, he will probably remember the illustrations and cartoons.

Because drawings leave a powerful image in the mind of a user, they provide a quick "index" to your reference manual. When the reader wants to look up a particular section of information, he will probably flip through the pages until he sees the illustration that accompanies the section he wants. It's much easier to remember a picture than words of text.

Whenever you use illustrations in your documentation, you must plan them just as carefully as you plan your text. In your detailed outline, indicate places where you want to include illustrations. Describe each drawing in detail, and put parentheses () around the description to remind you that you need to leave space for and create an illustration at that point.

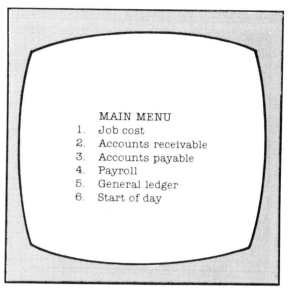

Fig. 6-13. This is the main menu for a small business system. It might appear at the beginning of the overview section of your documentation where you describe the general capabilities of your system. The first-level submenus might appear at the beginning of the overview for each specific section.

Think of your illustrations as a family. While each member of the family is a unique individual, there are many "family resemblances." Each of your illustrations will be unique, but there should be some characteristics in each that link it to the others. The "family resemblances" within your drawings can be subtle, but they should give your reader a sense of continuity.

Finally, remember that illustrations and cartoons have a purpose. They are not included in documentation manuals as decorations.

SAMPLE REPORTS AND OTHER PRINTOUTS

Your printer can be a useful tool when it comes to preparing documentation. You can have it print sample reports, program listings, and sometimes, screen images. Figure 6-14 shows a sample report.

By including actual printouts in your doc-

```
Sample Report: Vendor History Report. YTD

   Vend #      Vend Name                    YTD Paid
   1000        Acme Building Supply         $ 578.00
   1010        Andrews Printing             $5900.00
   1020        ******
   1030        Better Office Equipment      $7896.87
   1040        Collins Collections          $
   1050        Drew Graphics                $ 720.99
   1060        ******
   1070        Eagle Photocopy Services     $ 227.86
   1080        Fried Accounting             $9288.17
```

Fig. 6-14. This is a sample report. You can use sample reports as graphics within your text. Put them in the section that describes what the report does and how it is run.

umentation, you add authenticity to your work. Your reader will be far more impressed if you include a sample report than one that you hand lettered or typed on a typewriter. The mere fact that the documentation was prepared by a printer gives the reader the confidence that the program actually works and produces what your narrative says it can.

How to Get the Best Image from Your Printer

If you're going to use material that's printed by your printer, you should make sure that you get good quality printing. This is especially important when you plan to reproduce your work.

To get your printer working its best, start with a new ribbon. If you're like most of us, you're probably a little on the cheap side and like to get every last character out of a ribbon before retiring it. While this practice may be economical and practical for everyday uses, it will cheat you out of the dark easy-to-read characters you need for reproduction. You can save the old ribbon if you like, and put it back on after you've finished printing your documentation samples.

quick once-over. Make sure that you remove shreds of paper that have fallen into the unit, and fuzzies that have accumulated. Though it doesn't happen often, these foreign objects can cause printing problems. If you're familiar with a gentleman named Murphy, you know when those problems will occur.

The next thing you need to do to ensure quality printing is to invest in some good quality paper. The thin, inexpensive paper that's perfectly acceptable for everyday work has a tendency to absorb more of the ink from your ribbon than it should. This causes the printed image to be fuzzy or blurred instead of crisp and sharp.

Always use paper that is very white. You may not realize it, but there are many different shades of

As you're changing ribbons, give your printer a white paper on the market. The whiter the paper you use, the better the contrast will be between the black ink and the background of the paper.

Finally, when you actually begin printing, take a few minutes to make sure that your paper is inserted correctly and the printing is going well. Don't be afraid to hover over the printer like a mother hen. If you watch your work as it comes out, you can often catch errors before they become major problems and cause you to waste a lot of expensive paper.

REDUCTION PHOTOCOPIES: THE PROS AND CONS

You can save paper when you reproduce your documentation if you use a reduction photocopier to shrink large charts and printouts onto 8½ × 11 sized sheets of paper.

Documentation that fits on a standard page size is easier to package for distribution. It's also easier for the user to handle. He won't have to juggle with odd-sized pages.

The major disadvantage to using reduction photocopies is readability. The smaller your letters are, the harder they are to read. As letters shrink in size, the spaces between the letters also shrink. This can cause the letters to run together. Before you commit yourself to using a reduced copy of one of your charts or sample reports, make a test reduction. If it is difficult to read, stick with the larger paper required by the original.

A SUMMARY OF GRAPHICS TECHNIQUES

Graphic elements can make your documentation more interesting, more informative, and easier to read. Many times, a drawing or photograph will say a lot in a small amount of space. Graphics also give your reader a break from the monotony of reading page after page of solid text.

As you're planning your documentation, think of it as a total package—and include graphics within that package.

Chapter 7

Getting Professional Help

If you're feeling completely overwhelmed at the prospects of preparing documentation for your program, there is another approach you can take. You can ask someone to write your documentation for you.

When you ask someone to help you with your documentation, you want to be sure that both of you understand what's expected—right from the beginning. You need to decide exactly what your assistant will be responsible for and how you will compensate him.

For example, you may feel comfortable writing the narrative text and all the other written documents, but may feel uncomfortable with your ability to draw neat accurate graphics. In this case, you need to find someone who can handle the flowcharts and other graphics you want to include.

On the other hand, you may not want to tackle the writing, but feel comfortable doing the artwork. You'll need to find someone who can write.

Before you can approach someone and ask for help, you need to list exactly what that person must do. Whether it's graphics or text, you need to prepare a detailed list of all the items you will need.

The person who helps you prepare your documentation will need to know what you intend to provide him so he can complete his work. Since your assistant didn't write the program, you need to provide him with enough information to complete the portion of documentation you expect him to do.

If you're asking for help with the drawings, you might provide rough sketches or flowcharts. Your artist can then work from your sketches. If he has any questions (or can't read your writing), he should contact you BEFORE proceeding.

If you're asking for writing assistance, you can provide a rough draft that needs retyping and editing. If that's too difficult, you might be able to provide a detailed outline or detailed notes. Some programmers prefer to have their "ghost writer" interview them and get the information they need that way.

Whatever you decide to do, make sure your assistant understands clearly what he will be working with and how much work will be involved. If you're providing a rough draft, how much editing do you want your helper to do? Should he just correct grammar and spelling errors, or should he rewrite anything he doesn't like?

If you clarify things before starting the actual documentation, you'll have less headaches and fewer arguments later.

Whenever you're working with someone on a project, you need to keep in close contact. It's important to advise your helper of any changes you make in your program that could affect his work. It's also important to keep track of his progress. If you've promised delivery of your program by a certain date, you want to be sure the documentation will be complete in time.

Work for Hire

It's a good idea to draw up a formal agreement between yourself and the person who'll be helping you. The agreement should restate everything you discuss in your initial conversations including due dates, items included, and the form in which the material should be delivered. You should include a sentence in your agreement that says that the person is doing "work for hire." This means that when the work is completed, you own the copyright to it. (See Chapter 9 for more information on copyrights)

Payment and Other Forms of Compensation

You can pay your assistant in several different ways. Don't skirt the issue of payment. It only leads to bitter feelings. If you're not sure what your helper would like for payment, ask. Once you've heard his ideas, you can come up with a reasonable compensation plan that will be mutually agreeable.

If you're hiring a typist to retype your doc-umentation and correct any grammar, punctuation, and spelling mistakes, you will probably need to discuss a per-page compensation plan. The rates vary, but you can expect to pay as little as $1.00 per page—or much more.

Writers can be compensated in several ways. You can ask your writer to quote a price on the entire job. The price includes getting the work done by the due date you specify. You can also discuss a royalty agreement. If you've made an agreement with a publishing house, you can offer your assistant a portion of your royalties. Bear in mind that your helper may want a portion of your advance as well. Another form of compensation you may want to consider is based on time and materials. Your assistant will charge you based on the actual number of hours he spends on the work. The hourly rate should be agreed upon in advance. Your assistant would also charge you for any materials he needed to purchase in order to complete your assignment. The additional charges might include paper, type-writer ribbons, and photocopies. If you opt for a time and materials agreement, you may want to put a ceiling on the amount. That is, you may want to agree that you'll pay $5.00 per hour for the work, but no more than $500.

Artists usually have standard rates. There's a special rate for conceptual time and a different rate for board time. Conceptual time is the time it takes the artist to design a drawing. If you're including cartoons and border drawings in your documentation, the artist will need to spend some time thinking about what these drawings should look like. Board time is the time the artist actually spends drawing the flowchart or illustration.

Unless you have a dear friend who owes you a big favor, or can impress someone into slave labor, you're going to have to pay for any help you get. Good writers and artists aren't cheap. The prices you get may shock you at first. The amounts will depend upon the amount of work you want done and how quickly you need a finished product. The more help you can give your assistant, the less you'll have to pay. You'll get stuck paying a premium if you need the work done quickly.

After you've talked with a couple of people who could help you, decide whether it's worth the expense. It may be that you can do an adequate job on your own.

If you really need the help, but can't afford to pay what the people are asking, shop around. You may be able to find someone who'll work for less money and can get the job done to your satisfaction.

One last thought. Be sure you find someone you're comfortable working with. If you and your assistant are constantly butting heads over picky details or work styles, you'll both be miserable. If you're uncomfortable expressing your opinion because the person you hire seems to be such an expert, you'll be unhappy with the finished product. It won't sound like something you'd write, and you'll be uncomfortable showing it to people.

Checking on Someone Else's Work

When you write a program, you check the code carefully and then test the program to be sure it does what you think it should. When you get the drawings or writings from the person you've hired, check their work just as carefully as you check your own.

Be sure the work is technically accurate. You know your program better than anyone else. It's your responsibility to make sure that your assistant has gotten all the important information into the work and that the information is accurate.

Make sure the writing has the right tone. If you're documenting a game program, the documentation should be fun to read. If it's not, ask for a rewrite and tell your assistant what needs to be changed.

If you're having drawings done, be sure they look the way you envisioned them. If they don't explain what you don't like and have them changed.

You're paying for help. Be sure the finished product is what you want.

Essential Steps in Hiring Professional Help

When you decide that you need help writing your documentation remember to do each of the following:

Find the right people. This means that your assistants should be able to do the work and be able to work with you.

Clarify your working agreement at the beginning and get it in writing. Be sure to include what's expected of your assistant, what you need to provide, when the work is due, and what the compensation arrangements are. Make sure you state that you have a "work for hire" agreement.

Communicate with your assistant frequently. This keeps him up to date on changes and keeps you informed on his progress.

Check your assistant's work carefully. Be sure you get what you pay for.

Chapter 8

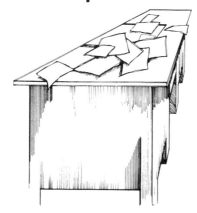

Putting It All Together

Now that your text and graphics are in their final forms, you have several decisions to make before you'll have an attractive and useful software package. You must decide upon the order in which the sections of your documentation will appear. You must also make decisions concerning the table of contents, the index, the binding, and the cover. Each of these elements deserves some careful consideration.

ORGANIZE YOUR MATERIAL

After you've written all of your documentation, you should put it into some logical order. The sequence you select will depend upon the audience to whom you're writing.

Regardless of who your intended audience is, your first section should be the program narrative. This gives your user a general overview of the program and its capabilities. It also alerts him as to what special hardware he needs and what other

requirements he must meet in order to successfully run your program. After you've supplied this, you can begin incorporating your text, flowcharts, and other parts of your documentation. If you're not sure which sequence is best, ask a disinterested individual. If what you've done makes sense to him, then it will probably make sense to your user.

THE PACKAGE CONCEPT

When all of the pieces of your documentation are in the correct sequence, you need to begin thinking of it as a package. This is the little bundle of goodies you're going to give to some unsuspecting user.

The package concept is a very important one. Up to this point, you've been working with the pieces of your documentation as unique and separate elements. Now, they've been combined into a single unit.

It's important for the package to have a unified

look, yet you need to preserve the uniqueness of each part of the documentation. This balance can be achieved by using several tried and true techniques.

Page Numbering

There are several options for numbering the pages of your documentation. The simplest is to number them sequentially from the beginning to the end. If your documentation package is bulky with lots of pages, you may want to treat each piece of the package as a separate section. The first page in each section can begin with the number one and then be numbered sequentially to the end of the section. If you select this option, you can avoid confusion by labeling each section with a letter and then prefacing the page number with the section letter-name (for example, A-1, B-1).

Some documentation packages work best with a combination of these two numbering options. The narrative section of the text and the step-by-step instructions could be grouped together and numbered from the beginning to the end. Flowcharts might be grouped separately in the back and called an appendix. The pages in the appendix would be numbered separately beginning with A-1.

Table of Contents

Virtually all documentation packages require a table of contents. This tells the reader two things. First, it indicates what is contained in the documentation. Second, it shows where to find things.

Your table of contents can be a very simple list of the sections into which you've divided your documentation and the pages on which each section begins. If the sections names are very general, you may want to include a brief list of the topics covered in each section. The topics can be run together in paragraph-like style, or listed in a column. You may find it beneficial to include the page numbers on which each of the key topics begins.

The table of contents page should be placed immediately behind the cover-sheet for your package.

Index

Most documentation packages do not include an index. This is not because indexes aren't useful; rather, it's because indexes are such a time-consuming nuisance to prepare. If you've prepared a bulky manual with lots of pages, you should give some consideration to preparing an index. Before you jump to the conclusion of "Why bother!" think of your user. Can he quickly locate the information he'll need? If your user will have to flip through many pages before he finds what he's looking for, an index should be given serious consideration.

Preparing an index isn't difficult. You'll need a couple of packages of 3 × 5 cards, a photocopy of your documentation, and a highlighting pen.

The first step is to read through your documentation page by page and highlight all the keywords. If the same keyword is repeated on several pages, highlight each occurrence.

After you've identified all the important words, take your 3 × 5 cards. Reread your documentation. When you find a keyword, write it on the top of a card and mark down the number of the page on which it appeared. Put only one word on a card. After you've prepared a few cards, you'll begin to find keywords for which you've already made cards. Find the card and add the new page number.

When you've finished, you'll have a stack of 3 × 5 cards with all the keywords and all the pages where those words appear.

Alphabetize your cards. Now you're ready to type your index. Type the word INDEX at the top of a sheet of paper, and then begin typing the words from the cards followed by the page numbers you listed. Leave a blank line each time you move from one letter of the alphabet to another so your reader can find things more easily. Soon, you'll have a complete, alphabetical list of all the important points you covered in your documentation and the pages where the reader can find them.

Section Separators

It should be easy for your reader to see where one section ends and another begins. There are two common ways to separate sections.

Page dividers provide a visual break between sections. A page divider can be a sheet of colored paper that's slightly thicker than the rest of the pages. A fancier divider might be a tabbed sheet with the section name printed or typed on both sides of the tab. If your documentation is thick, the tabbed dividers are much easier for your user to work with. With the simple page dividers, your reader will have to count the divider pages to get to the section he wants; with the tabbed pages, he can flip to the right section quickly.

A more dramatic way of separating sections is to print your documentation on colored paper. You might choose a different color for each section or choose two colors and alternate them.

Sometimes the two techniques are combined. The bulk of the documentation is printed on white paper and separated with tabbed pages. A single section is printed on colored paper. For example, you might print all of your charts or your step-by-step instructions on colored paper. Sometimes, the sections containing key commands and error messages are printed on colored paper.

If you decide to print a single section on colored paper, choose the one you feel will be most important to your user.

COVER OPTIONS

When you've taken care of all the inside details, it's time to consider the wrapper. The outside cover of your documentation is just as important as what's inside. The first impression your reader will have of the quality of your work will be from the cover.

You may think that if you hold the pages of your documentation together with a few staples or a rubber band, it will look like you concentrated your efforts on content rather than on the frills. Your reader, on the other hand, may think that you don't pay attention to details.

Judging what kind of cover will be attractive and appropriate is a very subjective task. Some people like Shaker-like simplicity. Other people are drawn to brightly-colored, flamboyant covers. The cover you select should be something you feel comfortable with, as well as something you feel is appropriate for the documentation you wrote.

BINDING OPTIONS

Package your documentation so that it is easy for your user to read and use. There are many different types of binders you can use to hold the pages of your documentation. The one or ones you choose will depend on the page sizes you include, how the material is to be used, and how much you want to spend on binding.

File Folders & Envelopes

The documentation you write for yourself can usually be kept in a manila file folder or a large envelope. Put all of the material for a program in a single place so you can find it quickly when you need it.

Data Processing Listing Binders

If you use fanfold paper for your program listings, you can store them in specially-designed binders that will allow you to keep them with the perforated borders and fanfolds intact. Figure 8-1 shows a typical program binder. You can keep many programs in this kind of binder and can add programs as needed. The programs can be separated

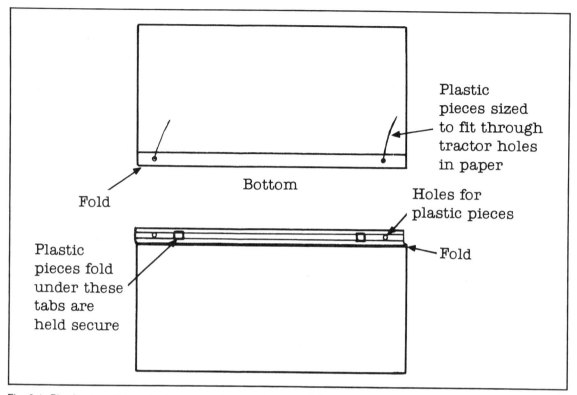

Plastic pieces sized to fit through tractor holes in paper

Bottom

Holes for plastic pieces

Fold

Fold

Plastic pieces fold under these tabs are held secure

Fig. 8-1. Plastic or cardboard binders are available that are specially designed to hold your program listings. They hold oversized listings neatly and can expand to hold about 5 inches worth of material.

by putting self-sticking tabs between each program listing. Use a spare piece of paper for the tab. This way, if you make changes to a program and completely replace one listing with another, you can reuse your tab.

Multipurpose Binders

Narratives, step-by-step instructions, and flowcharts that fit on 8-½ × 11 paper have many binding possibilities.

If you don't like punching holes in paper, there are several binders that will hold your pages in place with pressure-locks. These aren't as secure as ringed or permanent binders, but they are fine for small numbers of pages.

Text that's written on fanfold paper can be bound so that the reader flips the pages up instead of to the left. If you're producing the documentation yourself, this type of binder can save you time, because you won't have to split apart the fanfold paper.

3-Ring Binders. Still the most commonly used and most flexible document binder is the 3-ring notebook. These notebooks come in a wide range of sizes and colors. They can be made of heavy-duty paper, plastic, coated cardboard, and leather. Some are designed with pockets on the inside where you can stuff larger sheets of paper (such as oversized flowcharts).

When you insert your material into a 3-ring binder, you punch the holes on the left side of the page. If you have a horizontally formatted page (like a chart), punch the holes at the top. The publishing rule is that the reader should turn the book clockwise to view horizontal material.

There are many ready-made accessories for 3-ring binders. You can buy clear plastic sleeves to protect pages. The sections of your documentation can be separated with clear or colored tab pages. There are many 3-ring accessories you can use to make your documentation easy to read and give it a professional look.

GBC Binding. Many cookbooks and calendars are bound with GBC binders. These are plastic edges with horizontal strips that curl through rectangular holes punched in the pages. These binders are popular because they allow the bound pages to open flat. The binding strips come in several sizes and assorted colors. Check with a local printer to see if he has the equipment to do this kind of binding.

Heat Binders. Many businesses use heat binders to put together their proposals. The most common heat binders punch many small holes just inside the edge of the pages. A plastic spine with mini-spikes is then inserted from front to back through the holes. A second spine is heat sealed to the protruding spikes and the excess is trimmed. This is a neat looking binder and you can fit quite a few pages into documentation that is bound this way. The pages, however, will not lie flat when the book is opened.

One of the biggest disadvantages of either GBC or heat binding is that it requires special equipment. This equipment is a lot more expensive than a 3-hole punch. Also, pages that are bound with GBC or heat binders are difficult to swap. If you will be making periodic updates to your documentation and will need to add, delete, or replace pages, you should use a binding technique that is easier to update.

JUDGING A BOOK BY ITS COVER

What you say in your documentation is very important, but if your user isn't lured into reading what you've written, you've wasted your time. An attractive package will help entice your reader into looking at your work. If you're marketing your program to the general public, the packaging becomes even more important.

When you select a binding for your documentation, think carefully about how the material will be used. If you've written step-by-step instructions, make sure your reader can lay the book open on the table next to him. If you'll be providing periodic updates, make sure your user can easily insert the new pages.

Color is an important tool when it comes to marketing. It is also helpful when it comes to filing. Don't be fooled into thinking that your documentation will look more "official" if you put it in a black or brown binder. The only thing it will be is more boring! Also, it will quickly blend in with all the other black and brown binders on your user's reference shelf.

Choose a color that stands out. If red and yellow are too bright for you, choose a nice green or blue binder. They'll be more appealing to a user, and they'll be easier to find on a shelf.

Textured covers are lovely, but they cost a lot of money. If you plan to sell your program, you may be able to include the cost of a textured binder in the overall price of the program.

Colored tabs are attractive and helpful to the user. It's easier to remember that the step-by-step instructions are behind the yellow tab than that they're in section three.

The importance of packaging increases in direct proportion to the number of people who will be using the documentation. When you document a program for yourself, you can collect your documentation in very bland envelopes and file folders. Your Users' Group will be more impressed with your program if the documentation looks well-packaged as well as complete. The paying public is even more demanding. You will sell more copies of a mediocre program that has jazzy packaging than you will of an excellent program that has skimpy, poorly bound documentation.

Chapter 9

Evaluating Your Documentation

How good is your documentation? How do you tell the difference between good and bad documentation?

Your readers will be quick to tell you if you've written poor documentation; but many times they won't be able to offer constructive tips as to how you could improve it. There are ways you can evaluate your documentation before it goes out to users. When you take the time to develop and write an original program, don't sell it short by coupling it with bad documentation. Your documentation should enhance the value of your program, not detract from it.

It's often said that the value of a documentation manual can be measured by weight. The heavier it is, the better it must be. Using this measurement as a guideline, technical writers have produced huge tomes of text. Some have proved quite valuable as paperweights, others as doorstops. Most, however have been neatly stowed on a bookshelf where they gather cobwebs and dust.

Why are these volumes sitting idle? Quite simply, they're too bulky and cumbersome for a user to work with. The information they contain is buried within the text and is difficult to locate. Long hours of research and writing as well as printing costs have been wasted because the manuals aren't used.

When you write a manual, say what you need to say—in whatever space it takes. Don't stretch your text with a lot of unnecessary words just to fill up more pages.

PRETEND YOU'RE A USER

A common mistake made by programmers who write documentation is to say lots of things that don't help the user. For example, a user may be very interested in why you wrote a program, but couldn't care less why you wrote the program a particular way. If you write a narrative telling the history behind your program, talk about its purpose, not your technique. Don't try to impress the user by telling him how clever you are at programming. Most users won't care, and those that do can figure it out for themselves.

Easy Access to Details

Your users will have a variety of different backgrounds. Some will be new to computers and programs, others will be experienced programmers. Your manual must consider the needs of all its readers.

Both groups need to find the information they need quickly and easily. Help your users by providing them with an accurate table of contents, a detailed index, and lots of subheadings in your text. This gives your reader three ways to find information. It also lets advanced users skip over extraneous material and concentrate on just the details they need.

Users Don't Read Sequentially

When you read a magazine, do you read every page from the first to the last? Most people don't. Some start at the front and skim through until they find an article that interests them; then they read that completely. Others start at the back and read the ads and features before looking at any of the articles. Everyone has his own style of reading.

Your readers will tackle your manual in many different ways—to suit their own styles of reading. Don't assume that your users will read every page of your documentation, nor that they will read it from front to back.

Keep each section of your manual as self-sufficient as possible. Ideally, a reader should be able to read the sections of your manual in any order. Each section should contain all the critical information that the user needs to understand the material you present. This means that you'll need to repeat some information several times. Brief explanations of commands can be retyped whenever you use the command as a key element of your program. Lengthy descriptions can be typed once and then referenced in other sections.

It is imperative that you give your user a logical flow of information. Since you can't assume that someone reading section 3 knows what you presented in section 2, you must either reference section 2 or restate important information.

The Complete Reference

Your documentation should be complete. It should address and answer any questions that your users might have. Your users shouldn't have to interpret how your program works, what it does, or what the implications of various options are. Whenever you give your users a choice, explain what will happen in each case. Don't frustrate your user by making him learn by trial and error.

Provide warnings and tips. This information should be clearly marked in your documentation. Use bold type, underlining, arrows, boxes, stars, or any other technique that will call attention to the text.

Clearly explain how to get out of situations. For example, if your program has several subprograms, tell your user what to do if he accidentally runs the wrong program. Tell your user how to cancel out or abort processing in the middle of a program. If you don't, your user may hit the reset button only to find that your program no longer works because it didn't get the chance to end properly.

Realistically deal with the problems your user may encounter. Think of all the things that could go wrong. What happens if the user makes a typo and your program gets bad data? What if the user doesn't have all the information your program asks for? How long does it take to run your program? Assume that your user will have problems. Try to identify what they might be and then deal with them in your documentation. Remember, you won't be with your user to answer questions as they arise.

REMEMBER YOUR AUDIENCE

The first thing you consider when you prepare documentation is your audience. When you evaluate your work, make sure you haven't forgotten your audience as you prepared your work.

Addressing the Needs of Your Audience

What information does your audience want and need to know? Your documentation should both supply the right material and present it in the most convenient fashion to satisfy the needs of your readers.

If you've written multipurpose documentation, you should draw up a checklist of what each group of readers will expect. You'll probably duplicate items between groups. Check your list against your work to be sure you haven't left anything out.

Don't Make Assumptions

Unless you're writing to a very limited audience, you can't assume that your readers will have the same programming background that you do. Aspects of programming, logic, and coding techniques that are old hat to you may be brand new to your readers. If you breeze through material that you feel should be obvious your readers will either miss your point or feel frustrated and stupid. In either case, your documentation will fall short of its goal of being useful and informative.

Jargon, Buzz Words, and Inside Jokes

If you share your program and its documentation with your immediate Users' Group, you can get away with using jargon, buzz words, and inside jokes. In this case, your readers will both understand and enjoy the text. Once your program leaves that group, however, the jokes and jargon put roadblocks in the way of your users.

Programmers and users like to share new programs with their friends. Because of this, it's difficult to say who'll read your documentation once

you release it to your Users' Group. To play it safe, you should avoid using jargon and inside jokes in your text.

When you proofread your work, identify any buzz words you've used. Try to think of a way to substitute common English words for the term. If you must use buzz words or jargon, define the terms in a glossary at the end of your text.

READABILITY

The more difficult your text is to read, the fewer people will be inclined to read it. Readability has been the topic of much discussion in recent years. Studies have shown that most people don't like to be challenged by complicated text. Lengthy words and complex sentences make it difficult to extract important facts. Your readers won't want to play detective to figure out what you're trying to say.

You can simplify your writing and make it easier to read. To do this, you need to replace long words with shorter ones. Any word that's more than three syllables in length can slow a reader down. Long, complex sentences also pose problems for readers. When you find a sentence that's more than two lines of typed text, see if you can't break it into two shorter sentences.

Readability is measured by grade level. Several formulas have been developed to pinpoint how difficult a particular piece of text is to read. Just to give you an idea of how this applies to everyday writing, most magazines are written at between fourth and sixth grade levels. This means that an average student in the sixth grade would have no trouble reading the material. Technical manuals are written at a slightly higher grade level, but usually no greater than twelfth grade.

Why are magazines written at such a low grade level of difficulty? Because the publishers want people to read them! The publishers know that people don't like to struggle through text, so they make it easy for their readers to read their magazines.

If you'd like to see how difficult your writing is to read, take a random sample of about 100 words (about one page of text). Count the number of words having three or more syllables. (Exclude proper nouns, words with endings like "ing," "ed," "es,' and the like and hyphenated words like back-order.) Write down your count. Next, count all the words in the sample text. Finally, count the total number of sentences in the text. Divide the total number of words by the total number of sentences. This tells you the average number of words in a sentence. You're now ready to plug the numbers you got from your sample text into the formula shown in Fig. 9-1. When you complete the calculation, you'll know the grade level at which you write. If you're writing at tenth grade level or higher, you should make a concerted effort to simplify your writing.

GRAPHICS

If you include charts, screen images, or illustrations with your documentation, you should evaluate these in the same way you do your writing.

Readability Formula

1. Identify your sample text. Choose a paragraph or two that contains about 100 words.

2. Determine the Average Number of Words per Sentence. To do this, count the total number of words and the total number of sentences. Divide your word count by your sentence count to get your ANWS. (Note, count the total number of periods and semicolons to determine the number of sentences.)

3. Determine the number of multisyllablic words in your text. Words with more than three syllables are considered multisyllable. Exclude from your count all proper names, words ending with "es" or "ed," and two-word combinations like "bookkeeper" and "manpower."

4. Divide the total number of multisyllable words by the total number of words in your sample text to determine the Percentage of Difficult Words (PDW).

5. Add your ANWS number to your PDW number. Multiply the sum by 0.4. Ignore any numbers after the decimal point.

6. Your answer is the grade level at which you are writing. If the number is over 12, then you'd better be writing to a very sophisticated audience. Chances are, you need to make shorter sentences with easier words.

Fig. 9-1. If your documentation is too difficult to read, your readers won't bother. You can check the readability of your documentation by choosing a sample page or two and testing the text using this formula. (This formula is based on the FOG Index for Readability.)

The evaluation criteria is different, but the principle is the same.

Depending on the kind of graphics you include, you will need to check for different things. In general, however, your graphics should be usable and readable. Make sure that you've included them in a logical place in your documentation. Sometimes, it's better to put a flowchart in a section by itself. At other times, you'll want to include it as part of your text. Look at your graphics from your reader's point of view. Do they make sense? Do they help to clarify what you've said in the text? Do they answer more questions than they raise?

Graphics are included in documentation for a reason, not just for decoration. If your graphics are just taking up space, get rid of them. They won't help your reader, and they may even confuse him.

Charts

A chart should be pleasing to look at as well as informative. Check to see that each chart is centered on the page with ample space around the edges for your user to write notes on. Make sure you haven't squeezed too much on a page. If your chart looks cluttered, divide it between two pages.

While you're checking for an overall neat appearance, check the lines around the symbols, your connecting lines, and the dotted labeling lines. All should be straight and clean with no bumps and smudges. Carefully use an eraser or white liquid correction fluid to touch up any problem areas.

Proofread your chart. Make sure everything is labeled. Watch out for floating labels. These are labels that are out in the middle of nowhere. What usually happens is that you carefully letter the label and then forget to attach it to where it belongs with a dotted line. Finally, check each label for spelling errors. This step is especially important when you have lettered from right to left.

If you're using photo reduction to fit a large chart on a standard size page, check your labels for readability. As the letters shrink in size, they may tend to blur together. If you can't read the lettering, reletter your original chart with larger letters that are spaced further apart.

If your charts are neat and easy to read, your readers will be more inclined to spend some time studying them. Charts that are cluttered, messy, and difficult to follow are usually ignored.

Screen Images

There are two different ways to present screen images, and they are evaluated differently. Screen images that are hand drawn should have neat, clean lines. The lettering and graphic elements should be positioned exactly where they appear on a screen. Simple screen images can be drawn using squares. Use graph paper or templates to accurately draw your screen outlines. If you want to get fancy, you can purchase pads of television storyboard, paper from your local art store. The pages will have pre-drawn screen outlines so all you have to do is fill in the "picture."

If you've photographed your screens, make sure you can read what's on them. This is especially important if you plan to photocopy your documentation. It's better to include a hand-drawn sketch of a screen than a photograph that's blurred or hard to read. Printers use special techniques when they reproduce photographs. Don't be disappointed if photocopies of your screen images aren't as sharp and clear as the ones you see in books and magazines. As long as they're readable, they're worth including.

Tables

You may decide to put commands and error messages into tables. This collects critical information in a single spot. Both advanced users and beginners find tables helpful because they can turn to one or two pages for the answers they need.

Every table should have a name. The name

should be centered above the table. Each column in the table should have a heading. Separate the column headings from the rest of the table with a horizontal line or by leaving extra blank lines.

Spacing between columns is important. It helps tell the reader where one bit of information ends and another begins. The longest entry in each column should be separated from the next column by at least two spaces.

Naturally, the entries should line up horizontally. It's best to leave a blank line between entries, especially if some of the text spills over onto a second or third line.

If your table takes up more than one page, repeat the column headings on each subsequent page. Don't expect your reader to remember them.

Whenever a table is included on a page containing other text (for example between two paragraphs) separate it from the text. You can use horizontal lines above and below the table to do this, or you can enclose the table in a box.

Tables can be great time savers for your users providing they are easy to read, easy to find, and well labeled.

THE OVERALL PACKAGE

First impressions may not be lasting, but if the first impression isn't a good one, your documentation may not get a second look. How you package your documentation is just as important as how well it's written.

The type of cover or binding you use will depend on how many pages you have, how the documentation is to be used, and how much you choose to invest. There are some basic evaluation criteria that you can use when you select your packaging.

The outside cover or binder should protect the inside pages. Nothing looks less inviting to a reader than torn, dog-eared pages. If possible, get cover-sheets or binders that are slightly larger than your pages. If you bind your documentation with plastic or water-repellent covers, it will be protected from rain, snow, coffee, and soda. Covers like this can usually be wiped clean with a damp cloth, so they always look neat.

Color is important. Because it is very costly (or time consuming) to include color in your documentation, your text and graphics will probably be black and white. You can use a colorful cover to put some pizzazz in your documentation. Try to select colors that are bright and cheerful. Binders come in many assorted colors. Your local stationery store or printer can help you find colorful cover stock.

Don't overstuff a binder; if you do, pages will tear out. Your user will also have trouble turning pages while reading.

DIVIDE AND CONQUER

Most documentation manuals can be divided into sections. These sections might include:

Introduction
Narrative Description of Program
Step-by-Step Instructions
Sample Reports
Charts
Code Listing
Appendixes of Commands, Error Messages, and other reference information

Your documentation may not include all of the sections listed above, or they may not fall logically into that order. There may be other sections that you include.

Regardless of the size or number of sections you have in your manual, you must separate them so that the reader can find things easily.

A table of contents is a good place to start. Each section should be listed on your table of contents along with the number of the page on which it begins. If you like, you can expand your table of contents by including key topics that are discussed in each section.

Another simple way to separate one section from another is to put separator pages between sections. If you're using a three-ring binder, you can use tabbed pages. You can buy these pages in sets. Type or print the name of each section on the tab that precedes it. Be sure to put the name on both the front and back of each tab so your user can easily read from back to front or front to back.

A more dramatic way to separate the sections of your manual is to use colored pages. Because colored paper doesn't cost much more than white paper, this is an inexpensive way to add color to your documentation. Not only will it improve the overall appearance of your manual; it will perform a useful service for your readers.

There are several ways to use colored pages. The most carnival-like is to choose a different color for each section. A more manageable way to use colored pages is to use white sheets plus one other color. Alternate the colors so that the first section is printed on white pages, the second on colored pages, the third on white, and so on.

If you like the idea of using colored sheets but aren't quite ready to try the overall effect, you can call attention to a single section by putting those pages in a colored stock. For example, you might print all your charts on colored paper. Experiment with color until you find the technique that you like best.

It's important for your reader to be able to find information quickly. Use whatever technique works best for your documentation.

SUMMARY

Your documentation should be neatly presented in an attractive package. It should contain all the information your reader will need. Important details should be easy to find. Your reader will use your documentation more if he doesn't have to struggle to find the information he needs.

Good documentation is used on a regular basis. Bad documentation sits on a bookshelf and collects dust.

Chapter 10

Copyrights

If you ask ten people what a copyright is, you'll probably get twelve different answers. There are so many myths about what a copyright is that few people are able to accurately define it. Probably the most accurate definition you can get from the average person is that it is the little "c" with a circle around it that appears in the front of most books.

In fact, a copyright is a form of protection for you and anyone else who writes original documentation.

GETTING A COPYRIGHT

Copyrights are not reserved for the elite group of writers who have their work published and mass marketed. Anyone who writes original documentation can get a copyright for it. In fact, as soon as it's written it is automatically copywritten.

Do You Need a Lawyer?

The new laws say that as soon as you have finished writing your documentation, you own its copyright. You can register the work with the Copyright Office in Washington D.C. The registration procedure is very simple, so you shouldn't need a lawyer's help.

How Long Does Copyright Protection Last?

Copyright protection lasts for the life of the author and fifty years after his death. If there are coauthors for a work, then the protection extends fifty years after the death of the last surviving author.

Get the Facts

The United States Government has published an informative booklet explaining everything you need to know about copyrights. It's written in plain English so you won't need a lawyer to translate it for you. The booklet, shown in Fig. 10-1, is entitled *Copyright Basics* (Circular R1). To receive a copy,

Circular **R1**

Copyright Basics

Fig. 10-1. This circular is free. It's published by the government and tells you everything you need to know about copyright laws.

write to the Copyright Office, Library of Congress, Washington, D.C. 20559.

The information contained in the rest of this chapter has been largely adapted from that booklet.

COPYRIGHT DEFINED: WHAT'S COVERED AND WHAT'S NOT

A copyright is a form of protection offered to authors of original writing. It applys to both published and unpublished work. It gives the owner of the copyright (usually the author) certain exclusive rights. These include:

■ The right to photocopy or reproduce the work.
■ The right to incorporate parts of the work into subsequent writing.
■ The right to distribute copies of the work.
■ The right to sell, rent, lease, or lend the writing.
■ The right to transfer ownership of the copyright.
■ The right to publicly display the work.

Once you have written original documentation, you own the copyright to it. If someone wants to use your work or a large portion of it, they need to obtain your permission in writing.

What Can You Copyright?

You can copyright any written documentation text. This includes the narrative description for a program, step-by-step instructions, or the technical description of a program. Charts such as flowcharts or block diagrams can also be copyrighted. Even your program listing can be copyrighted. The screen images you photograph or draw can also be copyrighted.

The primary criteria for what you can copyright is that the work be original and tangible.

What Can't You Copyright

You can't copyright ideas. If you are thinking about writing a program and tell your idea to some-one else, you are not protected if that person rushes home and creates a program based on your idea.

Titles and single words can't be copyrighted. In order to prove that you were the author of something, there must be enough unique text or features to show that it was something you created.

Work-for-hire cannot be copyrighted. If you work for a company and write a program for that company or the documentation for a program, then you cannot claim the copyright ownership. The idea behind this is that the company is paying you to do the work for them.

You cannot copyright methods, procedures, systems, concepts, or processes. The way in which you code a program or the order of the logic cannot be copyrighted. This is different from the actual code you use or the narrative description you write.

The main concept behind copyright protection is to protect the authors of original work. Because of this, the work must be unique and tangible. Many people may approach a problem with a similar solution. For this reason, intangible things like method and processing cannot be copyrighted. The finished product as demonstrated in the actual code or narrative description, however, can be copyrighted because it is unlikely that two people would use exactly the same code or exactly the same text to create a finished product.

COPYRIGHT PROTECTION

A copyright notice must appear on all published copies of your work that are publicly distributed. You do not need to get permission from the Copyright Office of the United States to do this. If you forget to include the notice, you may lose some of your rights as the copyright owner.

The copyright notice is a "c" with a circle around it followed by the year in which you wrote the material and your name. For example:

© 1983 Barbara Spear

FORM TX

UNITED STATES COPYRIGHT OFFICE

REGISTRATION NUMBER

TX   TXU

EFFECTIVE DATE OF REGISTRATION

Month	Day	Year

DO NOT WRITE ABOVE THIS LINE. IF YOU NEED MORE SPACE, USE A SEPARATE CONTINUATION SHEET.

1

TITLE OF THIS WORK ▼

PREVIOUS OR ALTERNATIVE TITLES ▼

PUBLICATION AS A CONTRIBUTION   If this work was published as a contribution to a periodical, serial, or collection, give information about the collective work in which the contribution appeared.   **Title of Collective Work ▼**

If published in a periodical or serial give: **Volume ▼**   **Number ▼**   **Issue Date ▼**   **On Pages ▼**

2

a

NAME OF AUTHOR ▼   **DATES OF BIRTH AND DEATH**
Year Born ▼   Year Died ▼

Was this contribution to the work a "work made for hire"?
☐ Yes
☐ No

AUTHOR'S NATIONALITY OR DOMICILE
Name of Country
OR { Citizen of ▶ _____
Domiciled in ▶ _____

WAS THIS AUTHOR'S CONTRIBUTION TO THE WORK
Anonymous? ☐ Yes ☐ No
Pseudonymous? ☐ Yes ☐ No

If the answer to either of these questions is "Yes," see detailed instructions

NATURE OF AUTHORSHIP   Briefly describe nature of the material created by this author in which copyright is claimed. ▼

NOTE

Under the law, the "author" of a "work made for hire" is generally the employer, not the employee (see instructions). For any part of this work that was "made for hire" check "Yes" in the space provided, give the employer (or other person for whom the work was prepared) as "Author" of that part, and leave the space for dates of birth and death blank.

b

NAME OF AUTHOR ▼   **DATES OF BIRTH AND DEATH**
Year Born ▼   Year Died ▼

Was this contribution to the work a "work made for hire"?
☐ Yes
☐ No

AUTHOR'S NATIONALITY OR DOMICILE
Name of country
OR { Citizen of ▶ _____
Domiciled in ▶ _____

WAS THIS AUTHOR'S CONTRIBUTION TO THE WORK
Anonymous? ☐ Yes ☐ No
Pseudonymous? ☐ Yes ☐ No

If the answer to either of these questions is "Yes," see detailed instructions

NATURE OF AUTHORSHIP   Briefly describe nature of the material created by this author in which copyright is claimed. ▼

c

NAME OF AUTHOR ▼   **DATES OF BIRTH AND DEATH**
Year Born ▼   Year Died ▼

Was this contribution to the work a "work made for hire"?
☐ Yes
☐ No

AUTHOR'S NATIONALITY OR DOMICILE
Name of Country
OR { Citizen of ▶ _____
Domiciled in ▶ _____

WAS THIS AUTHOR'S CONTRIBUTION TO THE WORK
Anonymous? ☐ Yes ☐ No
Pseudonymous? ☐ Yes ☐ No

If the answer to either of these questions is "Yes," see detailed instructions

NATURE OF AUTHORSHIP   Briefly describe nature of the material created by this author in which copyright is claimed. ▼

3

YEAR IN WHICH CREATION OF THIS WORK WAS COMPLETED This information must be given in all cases.
◀ Year

DATE AND NATION OF FIRST PUBLICATION OF THIS PARTICULAR WORK
Complete this information ONLY if this work has been published.
Month ▶ _____ Day ▶ _____ Year ▶ _____
◀ Nation

4

See instructions before completing this space.

COPYRIGHT CLAIMANT(S) Name and address must be given even if the claimant is the same as the author given in space 2. ▼

TRANSFER If the claimant(s) named here in space 4 are different from the author(s) named in space 2, give a brief statement of how the claimant(s) obtained ownership of the copyright. ▼

DO NOT WRITE HERE   OFFICE USE ONLY

APPLICATION RECEIVED

ONE DEPOSIT RECEIVED

TWO DEPOSITS RECEIVED

REMITTANCE NUMBER AND DATE

MORE ON BACK ▶
• Complete all applicable spaces (numbers 5-11) on the reverse side of this page.
• See detailed instructions.
• Sign the form at line 10.

DO NOT WRITE HERE
Page 1 of _____ pages

Fig. 10-2. This is a sample of the application form you need to use to file your copyright with the government. You must use a government supplied form that you can get from the Copyright Office, Library of Congress, Washington, D.C. 20559. When you complete the form, send the original to the government and keep a copy for yourself.

DO NOT WRITE ABOVE THIS LINE. IF YOU NEED MORE SPACE, USE A SEPARATE CONTINUATION SHEET.

PREVIOUS REGISTRATION Has registration for this work, or for an earlier version of this work, already been made in the Copyright Office?

☐ **Yes** ☐ **No** If your answer is "Yes," why is another registration being sought? (Check appropriate box) ▼

☐ This is the first published edition of a work previously registered in unpublished form.

☐ This is the first application submitted by this author as copyright claimant.

☐ This is a changed version of the work, as shown by space 6 on this application.

If your answer is "Yes," give: **Previous Registration Number** ▼   **Year of Registration** ▼

5

DERIVATIVE WORK OR COMPILATION Complete both space 6a & 6b for a derivative work; complete only 6b for a compilation.

a. Preexisting Material Identify any preexisting work or works that this work is based on or incorporates. ▼

b. Material Added to This Work Give a brief, general statement of the material that has been added to this work and in which copyright is claimed. ▼

6

See instructions
before completing
this space

MANUFACTURERS AND LOCATIONS If this is a published work consisting preponderantly of nondramatic literary material in English, the law may require that the copies be manufactured in the United States or Canada for full protection. If so, the names of the manufacturers who performed certain processes, and the places where these processes were performed **must** be given. See instructions for details.

Names of Manufacturers ▼   **Places of Manufacture** ▼

7

REPRODUCTION FOR USE OF BLIND OR PHYSICALLY HANDICAPPED INDIVIDUALS A signature on this form at space 10, and a check in one of the boxes here in space 8, constitutes a non-exclusive grant of permission to the Library of Congress to reproduce and distribute solely for the blind and physically handicapped and under the conditions and limitations prescribed by the regulations of the Copyright Office: (1) copies of the work identified in space 1 of this application in Braille (or similar tactile symbols); or (2) phonorecords embodying a fixation of a reading of that work; or (3) both.

     a ☐ Copies and Phonorecords   b ☐ Copies Only   c ☐ Phonorecords Only

8

See instructions

DEPOSIT ACCOUNT If the registration fee is to be charged to a Deposit Account established in the Copyright Office, give name and number of Account.

Name ▼   **Account Number** ▼

9

CORRESPONDENCE Give name and address to which correspondence about this application should be sent. Name/Address/Apt/City/State/Zip ▼

Area Code & Telephone Number ▶

Be sure to
give your
daytime phone
◀ number

CERTIFICATION* I, the undersigned, hereby certify that I am the

Check one ▶

☐ author
☐ other copyright claimant
☐ owner of exclusive right(s)
☐ authorized agent of _____
       Name of author or other copyright claimant, or owner of exclusive right(s) ▲

of the work identified in this application and that the statements made by me in this application are correct to the best of my knowledge.

Typed or printed name and date ▼ If this is a published work, this date must be the same as or later than the date of publication given in space 3.

_____ date ▶ _____

👉 Handwritten signature (X) ▼

10

**MAIL
CERTIFI-
CATE TO**

Certificate
will be
mailed in
window
envelope

Name ▼

Number/Street/Apartment Number ▼

City/State/ZIP ▼

Have you:
• Completed all necessary spaces?
• Signed your application in space 10?
• Enclosed check or money order for $10 payable to *Register of Copyrights*?
• Enclosed your deposit material with the application and fee?

MAIL TO: Register of Copyrights, Library of Congress, Washington. D C 20559

11

You can spell out the word *Copyright* or use the abbreviation "Copr" if your printer or typewriter doesn't have the special copyright symbol.

You can abbreviate your name if you like, but it must be clearly recognizable as your name.

A copyright notice is not required on unpublished work. The Copyright Office recommends, however, that you include a notice on any unpublished work that leaves your hands. This can prevent accidental publishing without your permission. The way to mark unpublished material is:

Unpublished Work © 1983 Barbara Spear

Your copyright notice should appear in several places on your software package. It should be displayed on the first screen of your program. You should include it as part of the comment narrative that precedes your program code. The copyright notice should also appear on the labels of any disks or tapes you provide with your program. Finally, you should put a copyright notice on one of the first pages of your documentation and on any originally drawn charts that are included as part of the documentation manual.

Copyright Registration

Copyright registration is a legal formality. It puts on public record the details of the work to which you hold copyright ownership.

While it is not necessary to register a copyright, there are some advantages. Because it establishes your ownership on public record, it can protect you if you are ever sued and must go to court to prove ownership. In most cases, you would need to have your copyright registered to prove ownership in court.

To register your work, you need to get an application form from the Copyright Office, Library of Congress, Washington, D.C. 20559. Figure 10-2 shows an example of the application form.

Complete the application form. Send the completed form with a check or money order for $10 and a copy of the work you want to register to the Copyright Office at the address shown in the preceding column. Put everything into one envelope. This will prevent the three items from being separated. Do not send cash. Currency can get lost in the mail. Your $10 filing fee is nonrefundable. A separate fee is required for each work you want to register.

Be neat! Complete your application form in ink, or use a typewriter. The form becomes a part of the public record and will be reproduced. It should be legible and easy to photocopy.

Because the form becomes part of public records, you must use the actual form the Copyright Office sends you. A photocopy is not acceptable.

Plagiarism

Plagiarism is the unauthorized use of someone else's work. In school, teachers stress negative consequences for copying someone else's work. In a school environment, violating someone else's rights to ownership of a copyright is usually punished with a failing grade. In the real world, the consequences can be far more severe.

When you write original documentation, you spend a lot of time thinking of how best to explain what you need to say. When you finish, your work belongs to you. If someone were to copy everything you wrote, that person would be stealing from you. He would be stealing the time you took to write the work as well as the words themselves. In order to qualify as plagiarism, the work that is copied must be clearly that of another author.

How to Avoid Plagiarism

When you write documentation, give credit where credit is due. If you are writing a program for an accounts payable system and want to quote something from a textbook on accounting, give credit to the original author. Put the quoted text in quotations, and then use a footnote to tell the original source.

If you need to include more than a few phrases, you should secure permission from the original author. This is not difficult to do. Your letter should state that you want to license the use of the material for "one time use" and "for use only" so that the author understands that you are not looking for carte blanche privileges.

If the material you want to include is lengthy, include, a photocopy of what you want to use. This way, there'll be no misunderstanding.

The original author (or copyright owner) must give written permission before you can use the material as part of your documentation. Provide the author with a place to sign the agreement. As a courtesy, you could include a self-addressed stamped envelope. This will make it easier for the author to comply with your wishes.

Copyright Infringement

If you are accused of violating someone's copyright rights or if you feel that someone has violated yours, you need to protect yourself.

If your work has been copied without permission, you can file a complaint with the Copyright Office. Give all the facts. Describe the work that was copied and the author that copied your work, and include photocopies to document your complaint.

Regardless of who is in violation, you should contact an attorney who specializes in copyright law. He will be able to give you advice on how to handle the situation. Ask your regular attorney to recommend someone, or look in your local Yellow Pages for attorneys that specialize in this field.

Work-For-Hire

If you hire someone to write all or part of your documentation, you'll need to prepare a written agreement. Your agreement should state that the work being prepared is "work-for-hire." This means that you are subcontracting work and that the person is writing the documentation for you. If you don't do this, then the person who writes your documentation can claim original authorship and copyright ownership.

When two or more people collaborate to write documentation, both are considered original authors and the copyright ownership is shared.

SUMMARY

Copyrights protect original authors against plagiarism of their work. Copyright ownership takes effect immediately after the work is completed. Registration of a copyright is optional, but is inexpensive and easy to do. Registration can protect you if you ever need to go to court to prove copyright ownership.

Only tangible work can be copyrighted. Ideas, methods, single words, and short phrases cannot be copyrighted. Your program listing and any documentation you prepare can be copyrighted.

Copyright infringement and plagiarism are serious matters. If you need legal advice, go to a lawyer that specializes in copyright law.

When you ask someone to help you write documentation, it is important to establish—in writing—who owns the finished work.

Chapter 11

Are the Benefits Worth the Effort?

It takes time to prepare documentation. There's no getting around it. How much time it takes will depend on the type of program you've written and how much documentation you need to prepare, what kind of documentation you prepare, and how much practice you've had preparing documentation.

The kind of documentation you prepare is determined by the kind of program you've written and who your intended audience is. If you're writing to a technical audience like yourself or other programmers, you'll need to prepare technical documentation. If you expect your audience to be made up of users that only want to run your program, you'll need to write user documentation.

How much documentation you write will depend upon many factors. First, you need to decide how thorough you need to be. While it's pretty much a given fact that you can't prepare too much documentation, there's a lot of leeway between no documentation and one of everything.

Second, you must consider the type of program you've written. A utility program needs good technical documentation so the user can fully exploit the capabilities of the utility and take into consideration its limitations. An entertainment program doesn't require lots of technical documentation because the user won't be modifying and adapting the code. Good program narratives and step-by-step instructions, however, are very important for game documentation. Business programs need both kinds of documentation. The user must have a good understanding of the program as it was originally written and must be able to operate the program. The business user may also need to customize your program to suit his special needs, so it's important to provide the technical documentation that will let him do this.

Third, there's your audience to consider. If you know exactly who'll be reading your documentation, you can pinpoint which types of documentation will be most appreciated. If you don't know who your audience will be, you're almost forced into writing several different types of documentation in anticipation of what your audience might want to see.

In part, your audience is determined by the kind of program you write. Your audience is also determined by how you distribute your program. If you share your program with members of your computer club, you have a better idea of who's using your program and what their backgrounds are. If you mass market your program, you can only guess at who your users will be and what backgrounds they will have.

Third, time can be a factor. If you've written a program in June that displays fireworks on a screen, you don't have much time to prepare documentation and distribute your program before the Fourth of July. On the other hand, if you're writing a game or business program, you can deliver the finished product almost anytime. It's difficult to get your creative spirit to take time factors into consideration when thinking up new programs. Often, you won't think about a program that displays a decorated Christmas tree amid falling snow or a Chanukah minorah with flickering candles until the season is upon you. When this happens, you're stuck as far as time goes. Seasonal display programs don't require the extensive documentation that business programs do. When you write a business program, estimate how long the documentation will take to write and figure that into your expected completion or delivery date.

Some people enjoy writing documentation as a hobby. Those that do are usually employed as technical writers. If you tackle too big a project (especially on your first program), you'll probably become discouraged, disinterested, and never finish any of the documentation you start. If you build your documentation skills gradually, you'll begin to think of documentation as just another programming step. Start by mastering one kind of documentation;

then branch out and develop your skills in other areas. You may not be able to mass market your programs for a while, but when you are ready to enter the mass market, your documentation will be a positive reflection on your program.

Experience and practice are two key ingredients for preparing good documentation. The more you do, the easier it is.

If you've never written documentation before, start small. Begin by including a comment section at the beginning of your next program. You can then add subroutine names and comments to your program code as you go along. When you're done, print your listing and you'll have a good start for your documentation.

If you like to sketch a quick flowchart before you begin coding, start saving your charts. Keep them on file with your listing. Your freehand flowcharts may not be the neatest, but they'll give you something to work from if you ever decide to redraw them using some of the techniques described in this book.

Any other notes you make either before or during coding should also be saved. They may not be something you'd want anyone else to see, but they'll provide reference material if you ever need to prepare additional documentation.

As you become more comfortable writing the program notes and drawing flowcharts, you can try your hand at writing the various kinds of documentation that are described in this book. Tackle them one at a time, and don't rush yourself. The first pieces of documentation may not be Pulitzer prize winners, but that's not the point. Your first priority is to get the information down on paper. Next, you want to try to conform to each format as it's described in this text. When you're confident that you can get all your facts together and put them into the format you've chosen, then you're ready to worry about the writing specifics like style and tone.

Your first few attempts may sound very boring and dry to you. Don't let that bother you. There's nothing wrong with serious documentation that contains all the information the reader needs. As you become more comfortable writing, you'll be able to work into a more casual or humorous style. If you try to force your writing into such a style before you're really ready for it, then you'll probably leave out something important while you try to be casual.

TRADEOFFS

Documentation writing is full of tradeoffs. You trade your time for accurate and meaningful documentation. But that's just the beginning.

When you prepare a flowchart, you provide your reader with a graphic representation of your program. The chart is easy to read and doesn't take a lot of time to prepare; but a chart can never describe the way a program works in the detail that a narrative can. You must decide which is best for you and your user.

The type of cover you choose can make a big difference in the first impression your documentation makes. Your program will look like it's worth more if you bind its documentation in an expensive cover. Expensive looking covers don't come cheap, however. Is it worth the extra cost to put your documentation in a fancy binder? The same holds true for gimmicks. If you put your treasure hunt documentation in a cork-sealed bottle, it may be eye-catching, but it is not cost-effective or practical.

Sometimes, you can create very interesting and imaginative packaging for your documentation that isn't expensive. The tradeoff here is your creative time versus working with standard packaging materials. For example, if you're marketing a battle strategy game, you might design a cover that has the words TOP SECRET stenciled diagonally on it. The book might be sealed with an adhesive round wafer that the user would break before reading the documentation. This clever cover wouldn't be too expensive to produce, but you'd need to either draw the artwork yourself or explain to an artist exactly what you wanted. You'd also need to take some time thinking up this kind of creative cover design.

You'll always have to deal with tradeoffs as you write documentation. Many times you'll have to find a compromise between what you'd really like to do and what you really can do.

How Much is Enough?

When you mass market documentation, it's virtually impossible to write too much documentation (unless it doesn't say anything). But you don't want to make a career out of documenting a single program.

If you're writing documentation for yourself, you don't need to get fancy. As long as you include a good description of the program and highlight the important subroutines, you'll probably have enough documentation to meet your future needs.

"Run only" users need a good description of the program and accurate, easy-to-use instructions for running it. You'll overwhelm them if you include heavy technical documentation.

Members of your Users' Group are special people. They share many things in common with you. You probably have a pretty good understanding of what their background is and how much you can assume they know. When you write for this group, you can eliminate much of the explanatory material that your fellow users already understand.

The toughest group to write for is the general public. You don't know what they'll want or how they'll use your program, or what they know. When you've got a program that you feel has mass appeal, you'll need to spend a fair amount of time preparing comprehensive documentation. You should include some technical material, some descriptive narrative text, and some clear instructions for running the program.

Before you face the world with your documentation, ask someone to look it over and critique it. You may not like everything you hear. Don't take it personally. If there are problems with your documentation, you can thank your lucky stars that you got the opportunity to rework it before you presented it to others.

TAKE A CHANCE

Documentation can be a challenge, but it can also be fun. Try each of the documentation formats described in this book and find out which you like best. When you write good documentation, your programs are more complete and look more professional. If you know you'll be documenting a program, you'll probably be more careful to make notes to yourself as you design and code. By becoming more conscientious and organized when you create programs, you'll find you write better programs in less time. The notes you write as you go can keep you from making careless coding mistakes and having to do unnecessary recoding.

You don't have to be anybody special to write good documentation. All you need is a little organization, a little determination, a little practice, and this book to get you started.

Chapter 12

Documenting Your
Software for Publication

Other people may want to use the programs you write. These people can include your friends and other members of your Users' Group. As people express an interest in having your programs for their own use, you have two options. You can give them copies of your programs, or you can sell them copies. If you decide to give away copies, you may want to give just the code, or ask anyone that wants a copy to give you a blank tape or disk onto which you can copy your program. Otherwise, you could go broke just buying the supplies you'd need to make copies of your programs.

To expand your audience, you can advertise your program in Users' Group newsletters, and computer magazines. This lets more people know about your program, but the ads can get expensive. You must also take into consideration the expenses of packaging your software and mailing it to your customers.

One way to avoid a lot of personal expenses when marketing your program is to let someone else make the copies and do the advertising and distribution for you.

Commercial publishers are always on the look-out for good programs. These publishers are in the business of mass producing and mass marketing programs. They know how to do it right and how to do it cost-effectively.

You're probably thinking, "Who me? What publisher would want to look at my program?" You might be surprised! With the increasing number of computer owners, the demand for quality software programs exceeds the available supply. The "proven" authors are writing new books and programs all the time, but they can't keep up with the increasing demands of the market. Consequently, publishers are looking for new authors. Programmers who've written high quality original programs that answer the needs of computer owners. You could be one of those new authors—but first, you need to find a publishing house.

INTRODUCE YOURSELF TO A PUBLISHER

As with any business, there are right ways to do things and wrong ways. One of the most common mistakes made by aspiring programmers is to send their program code to a publisher for review and consideration for publishing. This is the wrong way to introduce yourself. Many programmers have been disappointed when their work was not published—and the publisher didn't return their materials.

Save yourself from this frustration by handling your introduction the right way. Begin by identifying one or more companies that might be interested in your program. Consider publishing houses, software houses, and computer manufacturers.

Choose one of the names on your list and send a letter like the one shown in Fig. 12-1. Your letter should help the publisher decide whether your program would be of interest. Here is a list of some of the things you should include:

1. The name of the program.
2. What the program is (for example, a stand alone program, subroutine library, a utility, or a system of related programs).
3. The major functions of your program.
4. Who will want to use your program.
5. What's unique about your program.
6. How your program stacks up against any direct competition.
7. The installation instructions and documentation that go with your program.
8. The experience you've had that qualifies you to write the program. (For example, you've been a ham radio operator for 10 years, so you write a program to teach Morse code to people who want to be hams.)

9. If anyone helped write the program, identify the other authors and explain their degree of contribution.

Your letter may be lengthy. That's okay. The publisher needs to know whether or not he should be interested in your program, and the more information you give him, the easier it is for him to make a decision.

Don't include any code listings or documentation manuals with your letter. If the publisher is interested in your programs, he'll ask you to send them, and will tell you exactly what you need to do.

SOFTWARE EVALUATION

Software is evaluated in many different ways. The evaluation criteria used by each publisher is usually quite specific, and the publisher can tell you how your program will be judged.

Evaluations take time. In order to properly examine your program, a publisher will assign one or more individuals to evaluate it. This evaluation can take anywhere from a few days to six months. It all depends on the publisher and the number of programs he has to evaluate when yours arrives. Be patient. It won't do you any good to pester the publisher. If anything, he'll get angry and reject your program before it gets a chance to be properly evaluated.

In addition to evaluating your program, the publisher will also evaluate your documentation. A good program with sloppy, inadequate documentation means a lot of work for a publisher. This drawback could put your program out of the running. To avoid this, you should know what publishers are looking for in documentation.

Figure 12-2 shows a checklist of sections and topics you should cover in your user's manual. As you can see, they span the gamut and provide the user with complete documentation. If you've omitted anything, make the necessary additions and corrections before you submit your manual to the

```
          Your Name
          Street Address
          City, State, Zipcode

          Date


          Name of Publishing House
          Street Address
          City, State, Zipcode

          Gentlemen:

          Would you be interested in publishing a program designed to teach people Morse
          code? I've recently designed and coded just such a program and believe it would be
          of interest to anyone who wanted to learn this form of communication. Potential
          users would include scouts, aspiring radio amateurs, or anyone interested in radio
          communications and code languages.
              The program would be contained on a 5 1/4 inch diskette and would come with
          complete documentation.
              There are four main parts to the program. First, it introduces the user to the
          sounds of Morse Code and uses keyboard and stund options to teach the user the
          various characters used in code communications. A second section contains sam-
          ple exercises to help the user hear code messages which contain "strings" of
          characters. The third section gives the user practice sending predefined messages
          by using specially designated "dot" and "dash" keys. The last section concentrates
          on speed. Exercises help the user build speed in both sending and receiving code.
              The user manual describes the program and its exercises in detail. It also
          shows how the user can build a simple "code key" and interface it with his keyboard
          input. A glossary of code terms and common code abbreviations is included in the
          back of the manual.
              If you feel you might be interested in publishing a program of this type, please
          let me know. I'd be pleased to send you a sample disk, code listing, and a copy of the
          documentation manual for your review.

          Sincerely yours,


          Your Name
```

Fig. 12-1. This is a sample of the kind of letter you might send to a publisher to see if he's interested in your program. Put lots of details in your letter, but don't send a copy of your program or its documentation.

Topics for a Users Manual

1. Introduction

    a. Overview
    b. Features and benefits
    c. Equipment requirements

2. General Narrative

    a. Description of program functions
    b. Explanation of general objectives

3. Program Instructions

    a. First-time set-up instructions
    b. General start-up instructions (sign on etc.)
    c. Step-by-step instructions for each program
    d. End-program instructions: normal and abnormal
    e. How to correct mistakes

4. Graphics

    a. Sample screens
    b. Flowcharts
    c. Sample reports

5. Messages and Commands

    a. Prompts and error messages alphabetically
    b. Commands alphabetically

6. Index

Note: remember to include subheadings and figure captions

Fig. 12-2. Publishers are looking for program documentation that is accurate, readable, and complete. Here's a list of some of the things they look for.

publisher. The checklist also suggests the possible order you might use for organizing your documentation.

If your documentation is complete and technically accurate, the publisher will be more likely to accept your program for publishing. There are two pluses for good documentation. First, it implies that you've paid attention to details in your program. Someone who writes accurate, detailed documentation is usually detail oriented. Second, the less work a publisher will have to do to get your work in shape, the happier he is. The less time he needs to spend fixing your documentation, the quicker he can get it on the market and the less he'll have to invest in it.

Rejection Letters

Rejection is something we all face throughout our lives. We don't get into the school we want to attend; we don't get the promotion we deserve or the job for which we apply. Each of these disappointments hurts for a while, but somehow life goes on.

The first rejection letter from a publisher, though, is a different matter. Most people take it as a personal insult—an indication that they, not their program, have been rejected. This is silly. There are many reasons a publisher may reject your proram. Unbeknownst to you, the publisher may have just contracted with someone else to write a similar program. The publisher may also feel that your program isn't suitable for his customers. It's not necessarily a negative reflection on either you or your program!

Take rejection letters in stride. As soon as you are rejected by one publisher, send a letter off to another. If the first publisher gave any reasons for rejecting your program, or suggestions for improving it, think about them. Decide whether or not to incorporate them; then continue to look for a publisher for your program.

Remember, once your program is published and starts selling, you'll have the last laugh on anyone who didn't take advantage of your offer! You can laugh all the way to the bank!

Acceptance Letters

Oh Happy Day! You go to your mailbox, and there's a letter from a publisher expressing interest in your program. After you gleefully tell everyone you know that you're about to become a published author, take a few minutes to study the letter.

It's important to know what the publisher wants you to do. Do exactly as you're told. This is not a time to get creative.

If the publisher wants you to send documentation and code listings, carefully read the instructions on how to submit them. Most publishers have a standard set of conventions you'll have to follow when you submit your work. This makes their job easier, and they'll do a better job at publishing your program.

If you don't understand what you're supposed to do, call or write to the publisher for clarification. Don't guess.

DOCUMENTATION IN MANUSCRIPT FORM

Every publisher has his own rules for manuscript preparation. Here are some general tips that you may find helpful.

1. Be sure to put a fresh ribbon in your printer or typewriter. Publishers get irritated when they must read pale gray text. With all the reading, they don't need the added eyestrain. Help them out by making your work easy to read. They'll return the favor by helping you.
2. Send everything at once. Get your documentation manual prepared and send it in one large package. This prevents pages from being separated and lost. If you like, you can invest in a 3-ring binder and put everything in the binder. Use tabbed pages to separate the various sections.
3. Double space your text and leave wide margins. This gives an editor room to make changes if necessary.
4. Be sure all illustrations, charts, and screen

images are labeled and have captions. The labels tell the layout artist where graphics should be inserted in the text. The captions will help your reader understand what the graphic is all about.

5. Put your documentation into the order you want it presented to the user. Include a table of contents (without page numbers) to identify topic or section headings.
6. Program listings should be printed on clean white paper using a new ribbon so that they can be reproduced.
7. Photographs should be sharp and clear and in most cases should be black-and-white 8 by 10s.
8. Make last minute corrections in pencil and print your changes.

MARKETING QUESTIONNAIRES

You may be asked to complete a questionnaire and submit it with your manuscript. Traditionally, this questionnaire gives you the opportunity to provide information to the publisher's marketing department so that they can advertise your program.

Take a few minutes to think about your answers before you write them down. Your input is important. The marketing staff will consider your opinions when they plan a marketing strategy for your program. You may be able to give them ideas and tip them off to features in your program that might otherwise go unnoticed.

CONTRACTS AND ROYALTIES

Most publishers require you to sign a contract before they will publish your program. This contract gives them the right to publish your work and details the financial arrangement as well as other commitments both of you agree to.

Publishing contracts are pretty standard. Read your contract carefully and make sure you understand everything it says. If you have questions, ask the publisher to clarify what you don't understand.

Authors (and programmers) are usually paid based on the number of copies of their program that the publisher sells. The term for this income is *royalties*. Royalties are usually paid two to four times per year based on the sales of the last quarter or six months. You won't get a weekly or biweekly check, but the one you get will usually be substantial.

You get a percentage of the selling price of your program. The publisher may ask you to help him price your program, or he may decide to set a price on his own. The price will depend on the kind of program, the number of features it has to offer, and the prices of competitive programs already on the market. If you wrote a game program, and the competition was selling similar games for $30, you wouldn't want to have yours priced at $60 unless there was something really special about it.

Sometimes publishers will give you an advance when you sign your contract and/or when you submit your program and its documentation. This is usually an advance against anticipated royalties. When you get your first royalty check, the amount the publisher advanced you is usually deducted and the check is for the balance.

One word of caution. Don't expect to become a millionaire overnight. There's a big difference between program sales and bestseller novel sales. The number of potential customers is usually smaller (especially if your program is machine specific). Of course, there are a few programs that sell lots and lots of copies, but for everyone that does, there are hundreds that sell only a few hundred or a few thousand copies.

VANITY PRESSES

If you're getting a healthy collection of rejection letters, it's time to try a new approach.

First, try to determine why the publishers are not champing at the bit to publish your program. Is it the program? The documentation? The application? Are you approaching the wrong publishers?

If your program and documentation are good, and the application would appeal to a large number of people, you can consider publishing your software on your own if you can't get a publisher to accept it.

The cheapest way to do this is to duplicate your documentation and program listing and market the program by putting ads in Users' Group newsletters and computer magazines. This is a good way to begin. It gives you a chance to "test the market" and see if there is a demand for your program.

If you get a lot of responses, and people seem interested in your program, you may want to give your documentation a professional look. You can do this by hiring a publisher to print and bind your documentation. Publishers who do this kind of work-for-hire are known by the term *vanity presses*. All this means is that you're footing the bill to have your work published.

The difference between a vanity press publisher and other publishers is who takes the financial risk. Most of the publishers to whom you'll send letters will be assuming the expenses of typesetting, printing, and binding your documentation. If you approach a vanity press, you'll be expected to pay the publishing expenses.

This may seem like an expensive proposition, but if your program and its documentation are good, you can price your work so that you more than recoup the initial publishing costs.

SUMMARY

There are many ways to publish your programs and documentation. You can do it yourself and handle all of the advertising as well. You can submit your work to a publishing house and let them do the publishing and advertising, or you can contract with a vanity press where you pay the expenses, but they take care of the actual work that goes into producing a bound manual.

Chapter 13

Books for Further Reading

This list contains books you may want to review if you want more information on a specific topic. For example, if you'd like to know more about writing in plain English, you should find one of the many books written by Rudolf Flesch. He specializes in this topic and his work is both helpful and enjoyable to read. S. I. Hayakawa has written many books on the science of language. His specialty is talking about how and why language works the way it does. If you'd like to know more about how your words and the way you put them together produce specific effects on people, you should look up some of his works.

Some of the books and articles listed in this bibliography may seem very academic and too detailed for you. After all, your main goal is to produce readable and useful documentation. Your main interest is probably in developing and coding programs. If you're looking for a good general reference book that will help you check your work for grammatical errors, you should definitely get a copy of Chopeta Lyons' *Discover Writing*. Unlike most traditional grammar books, this book shows you quick short-cuts to editing your text. It wasn't written for children just starting to learn grammar. It addresses the common problems and slipups experienced writers make.

There are many other wonderful books on the market. Take a walk through the aisles of your local bookstore or public library if you need more information on a specific topic. You'll find specialty books on almost every topic that's been discussed in this book.

IBM Software Submission Guide
International Business Machines Corp. 1982.

Pocket Pal.
International Paper Company
New York, NY 1970

A Manual for Writers
Kate L. Turabian
University of Chicago Press
Chicago, IL 1973

The Language of Argument
Daniel McDonald
Harper & Row, Publishers
New York, NY 1980

Reference Manual for Office Personnel
House and Koebele
South-Western Publishing Co.
Cincinnati, OH 1970

The Famous Andrew Swanfeldt Crossword Puzzle Dictionary
Thomas Y. Crowell Company
New York, NY 1977

Language in Thought and Action
S. I. Hayakawa
Harcourt, Brace & World, Inc.
New York, NY 1964

How to Write Plain English: A Book for Lawyers & Consumers
Rudolf Flesch
Harper & Row, Publishers
New York, NY 1979

Printing Layout and Design
Delmar Publishers, Inc.
Albany, NY 1955

Designing with Type
James Craig
Watson-Guptill Publications
New York, NY 1971

Editing by Design
Jan V. White
R. R. Bowker Company
New York, NY 1974

Microprogrammers Market 1984
Marshall Hamilton
TAB Books, Inc.
Blue Ridge Summit, PA 1984

Illustrated Dictionary of Microcomputer Terminology
Michael F. Hordeski
TAB Books, Inc.
Blue Ridge Summit, PA 1978

Computerists Handy Databook/Dictionary
Clayton L. Hallmark
TAB Books, Inc.
Blue Ridge Summit, PA 1979

Data Dictionary Systems
H. Lefkovitz
QED Information Sciences
Wellesley MA 1977

Documentation Standards
Max Gray and Keith R. London
Auerbach
Philadelphia, PA 1969

"Why We Still Have So Little Technical Documentation"
E. H. Weiss
Infosystems, May 83 pp 88-89

Grammar and Good Taste: Reforming the American Language
Dennis E. Baron,
Yale University Press
New Haven and London 1982

Pocketbook for Technical and Professional Writers
Earl G. Bingham
Wadsworth Publishing Company,
Division of Wadsworth, Inc.
Belmont, CA 1982

How to Write Computer Manuals for Users
Susan J. Grimm
Lifetime Learning Publications,
Division of Wadsworth, Inc.
Belmont, CA 1982

Technical Writing
John M. Lannon
Little Brown & Company
Boston, MA 1982

Discover Writing
Chopeta C. Lyons
Prentice-Hall, Inc.
Englewood Cliffs, NJ 1984

Essentials for the Scientific & Technical Writer
Hardy Hoover
Dover Publications, Inc.
New York, NY 1982

Appendix A

Let's See How the Pros Do It!

One of the best ways to learn how to prepare quality documentation is to study documentation that professionals have written. Take a careful look at the user's manuals that support your computer and the software you have. How are the manuals put together? What type of binding do they use? How are the topics presented?

Instead of looking to your manuals for operational information, look to them as a documentation reference. Eventually, you'll find that you like some techniques better than others. Incorporate these techniques when you write your own documentation.

GENERAL OBSERVATIONS

This appendix contains reprints of pages from the instruction manual for a ColecoVision game cartridge. The techniques that are used are pointed out and analyzed, and the merits of these techniques are described in detail. When you study other documentation booklets and manuals, you may want to make notes in the margins when you find techniques that have been used to make the manual more valuable to the user. Before going into the specific features of the instruction booklet, lets make some general observations.

Size

Note the size of the pages. The booklet is compact. It was specifically designed to fit in the box that contains the cartridge. If the booklet were printed on standard 8-½ by 11 paper, it would have to be folded to fit in the package. If your program comes on a disk, you may want to put your documentation on small paper so it fits neatly in the package.

Writing Style

Note the way the instructions are written. The writers use plain English. The sentences are simple and easy to read. The vocabulary that's used is made up of common words and familiar terms. Some baseball slang is even included to help set the tone and get the user into the spirit of the game.

Layout

There's a lot of information in this booklet, but the pages don't look cluttered and information is easy to find. This feat is accomplished by structuring the text into a special layout that can handle lots of information.

Important section headings are set apart from the rest of the text by horizontal rules. Extra line spacing is left between the end of one piece of text and the subheading for the next piece. All subheadings are printed in a boldface type for emphasis. Important facts and features are pointed out through the use of numbered lists. These techniques help draw the reader's attention to the important points in the text.

Graphics

There are three kinds of graphics that are included in the booklet. First, there are the stop-action drawings of baseball players. These drawings are framed with a thin rule that has rounded corners. The stop-action drawings are used to set the mood and add realism to the game. Each drawing is carefully positioned in the text so that the picture depicts the topic that's being discussed.

The second type of drawing that's included in this booklet is an informational drawing. It depicts a special accessory is used with the game called a Super Action Controller. Each part of the controller is identified so that when its function is described in the text, the user can quickly determine what's being referenced. This instructional drawing is framed in the same way as the stop-action drawings. This helps to unify the artwork and provide a continuity throughout the booklet.

The third type of graphic that is included in the booklet is the screen image. This shows the user what he can expect to see on the screen when the game is played. The screen images are framed with a thin rule that has squared off corners. This is done to show that the screen images are different from the other artwork. Their function is different. By using the thin rule, the screen images are tied into the other graphics, and the continuity is maintained. By using square corners instead of rounded ones, they are distinguished from the other artwork.

The artwork in the book, like the use of format techniques, helps pull the pages together into a unified booklet. They look like they belong together as a group—even before the user begins reading the text.

The Sequence in which Material is Presented

The text sections of the booklet are presented in a logical, easy-to-follow sequence. Knowing that most game players like to dive right into the game, the editor has provided instructions for starting the game at the very front. The options the user will have when the game is started are discussed in the first section of the booklet.

The next section explains the use of the Super Action Controller accessory. This is at the front because the user will need to install a special keypad overlay to play the game effectively.

After the user knows how to start the game and what equipment he will need, the game action is described. First, the user learns about offensive play; then he learns about defensive play.

Towards the back of the booklet, the rules for scoring and winning the game are explained. These become important after the user has learned how to play the game.

The back pages also provide the user with tips on how to improve his game play. Until the user has experimented with the basics, he isn't ready to worry about improving his performance!

The very last text that is presented is the marketing and legal information. While this information is important and needs to be included, most game players aren't interested in reading through that when they first open the package.

Putting it all Together

This booklet reflects the efforts of professional writers, artists, designers, and editors. Even though this is an operating manual for a game, much careful thought and planning has gone into its preparation. When you document a game, you owe it to your user to put the same amount of effort into that documentation as you would put into the documentation for a business, scientific, or utility program.

THE SPECIFICS

Coleco designed every detail of the booklet carefully in order to produce documentation that was appealing, easy-to-use, and complete.

The Cover

The cover is the first introduction the user has to the game. It must be eye-catching and capture the flavor of the game in addition to stating the name of the game and the contents of the booklet.

In this case, several elements contribute to capturing the spirit of the game. First, the picture shows stop-action pictures of several baseball players. The action element is further stressed by the use of italic type on the words *SUPER ACTION*. Type is used a second time to create a special effect. The word BASEBALL is put in a special typeface that looks like the felt lettering found on baseball caps.

The cover clearly indicates that the game is a COLECO product and is designed for use on either ColecoVision or the ADAM Family Computer System. The user is even told what special accessories he will need to play the game (SUPER ACTION CONTROLLERS).

The short narrative near the bottom of the cover helps to set the action packed mood of the game.

Booklet reprinted courtesy of Coleco Industries, Inc.

135

Pages 2 and 3

These pages tell the user what he needs to do before beginning game play. The main topic is set apart from the rest of the text by two horizontal lines. This style technique is followed throughout the booklet. Major subtopics are printed in large bold type.

First, the user is told how to install the game. He is then told what to expect immediately after the game begins.

Horizontal lines border major topics

Start up instructions

Warning done in large dark type

GETTING READY TO PLAY

MAKE SURE THE COLECOVISION® CONSOLE IS OFF BEFORE INSERTING OR REMOVING A CARTRIDGE.

PLAY BALL!

Action drawing continues cover theme

Mood setting subheading

Choose your challenge.

Press the Reset Button. The Title Screen appears on your TV. Wait for the Game Option Screen to appear. It contains a list of game options, numbered 1-6:

SPRING TRAINING

1. **Batting Practice — One Player**

   Bat against every type of pitch. Knock that ball into the field, then prepare for the next pitch. If you hit the ball, as soon as it stops another pitch is thrown. If you don't hit the ball, another pitch is thrown as soon as the ball leaves the screen. (Batting Practice plays at Skill Level 2.)

2. **Fielding — Skill 1**

   The computer sends random fair balls to the field for practice when you press any number key. Repeated presses give you repeated fair balls. Learn to stop grounders and catch fly balls. Practice double plays. There are no base runners to confuse your game. Get it down!

3. **Fielding — Skill 2**

   The same as Skill 1, only you must position your fielders more precisely to make them grab the ball. If an infielder

2

136

The action mood is continued from the front cover through the use of a stop-action drawing of a player. The drawing is boxed with a thin rule that has rounded corners. You'll see that all other drawings are contained within the same kind of frame. Did you also notice that the player that's featured in the drawing is the same as one of the players shown on the cover?

touches a moving ball without catching it, the ball can bounce away.

4. **Pitch and Bat — Two Players**

One player pitches, the other hits. There's no fielding, base running or score. It's exhibition practice before the season begins!

HEAD-TO-HEAD™ BASEBALL

5. **Skill 1**

Here it is — two-player competition in our national pastime!

6. **Skill 2**

The same as Skill 1, only you must position your fielders more precisely to make them grab the ball. If an infielder touches a moving ball without catching it, the ball can bounce away.

Select your game option by pressing the corresponding number button on either controller keypad.

When playing Game Options 1 through 4, you can return to the Game Option Screen any time by pressing "Return" (Key #). When playing HEAD-TO-HEAD™ Game Option 5 or 6, press the **Reset** button instead.   Instructional note

One-Player Games
Use the Port 1 controller.

Two-Player Games
Player 1 (home team — Red) uses the Port 1 controller. Player 2 (visitor — Blue) uses the Port 2 controller. Player 2 bats first.

NOTE: If the horizontal and vertical adjustments on your TV are not properly set, the ball might disappear in an upper corner of the screen. The outfielder can still retrieve the ball, however, to complete a play.   Equipment reminder

3

This page explains how the Super Action Controller is used to play the baseball game.

A drawing identifies the parts of the controller and indicates how the overlay is put onto the controller. The special features are then described in the text. A number is associated with each feature. This makes it easier for the user to find the parts and their functions.

**Special
equipment
required
for game**

**Diagram shows
labels for important parts.
Note that this drawing
is boxed like others
for consistency.**

**How special
equipment
works with
game**

USING YOUR CONTROLS

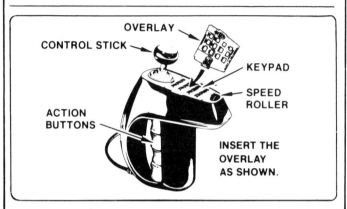

OVERLAY

CONTROL STICK

KEYPAD

SPEED ROLLER

ACTION BUTTONS

INSERT THE OVERLAY AS SHOWN.

1. **Control Stick:** Use your Control Stick to modify a pitch, move fielders or swing the bat.
2. **Keypad:** Press only one Keypad Button at a time. Use Keypad Buttons to select pitch speed, to permit base runners to steal, to throw a pick-off, or to return the ball to the pitcher.
3. **Speed Roller:** Move your base runner forward by rolling the Speed Roller to the right. Move your base runner back by rolling the Speed Roller to the left.
4. **Action Buttons:**

   Defense—(Team in the field)

   As pitcher, you choose the type of pitch with the Action Buttons. Use the color-coded Pitch Selection area on the left side of the overlay. The color of the pitch type on the overlay corresponds to the color of the Action Button. Once the ball is hit, select the player you want to field that ball. For details, see the appropriate section following.

   Offense—(Team at bat)

   When your team is at bat and you have men on base, you use the Action Buttons to select which base runners are to run.

4

This page is the first page that describes the actual game play. Again, a stop-action drawing is used to continue the mood of the game. In this case, the drawing also tells the reader what aspect of game play is being discussed.

OFFENSE (Team At Bat)

BATTING

Step up to the plate!

Rub your fingers in the dirt and grab that bat. Ready? This pitcher's got some stuff. Now you've got to hit it! Your Control Stick controls the bat. Swing for low pitches by pressing the stick down (toward you). Swing for high pitches by pressing the stick up (away from you). Press the Control Stick left or right for those pitches thrown right at your belt buckle. Watch for curves and sliders. Don't swing for the stars. And whatever you do, hit that ball! (For Batting Tips, see page 13.)

Run!

Make your batter run by rolling the Speed Roller. If you want the batter to run beyond first, press the blue Action Button as you roll the Speed Roller. Release the button when you want him to stop.

Batter Up!

The play is over when all runners have scored or are standing on their bases, and the ball is back in the pitcher's glove. Throw the ball back to the pitcher by pressing "RETURN" (Key #) on the keypad.

Next hit.

If you want your batter and/or your man on base to run, you must press the appropriate Action Button(s). Check the color-coded player locations on the Fielder & Runner Control

5

Subtopics

Graphic shows topic being discussed & reinforces theme

Pages 6 and 7

Page 6 shows an actual screen image. This helps the user translate the action in a real baseball game to the images he'll see on the screen. Because this is a different kind of graphic element than the drawings, the corners have been squared off. This helps to subtly distinguish the screen image from the other drawings in the booklet.

More offense topics are discussed on these two pages.

Screen image - note square corners this distinguishes the screen image from a drawing

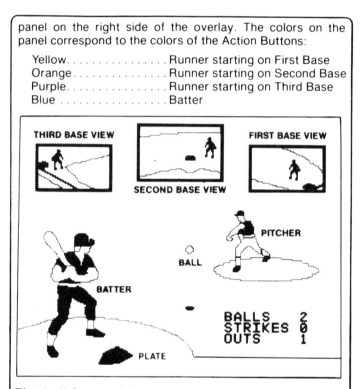

panel on the right side of the overlay. The colors on the panel correspond to the colors of the Action Buttons:

Yellow . . . . Runner starting on First Base
Orange . . . . Runner starting on Second Base
Purple . . . . Runner starting on Third Base
Blue . . . . Batter

THIRD BASE VIEW   SECOND BASE VIEW   FIRST BASE VIEW

BATTER   BALL   PITCHER   PLATE

BALLS   2
STRIKES   0
OUTS   1

The ball is caught.

If your runner is away from the base when a line drive or fly ball is caught, the runner must return to the base (tag up) before running on. Press his Action Button and roll the Speed Roller to the left to tag him up. Then take stock: are the infielders waiting for your move? Maybe hold off running until the next hit.

Take heed: if your runner reaches or passes the next base, he **cannot** return to his original base. If a fly is hit, protect your runner by holding up before reaching the next base to see if the fly is caught. For a runner from third to score when

6

140

a fly ball is hit, he must cross home after the ball lands without being caught, or after tagging up at third if the ball is caught.

No Passing.

Caution! No runner can pass another on base or on the basepath. Your first man must run forward before other runners can follow.

Keep your men a safe distance apart. On first and third, runners can block each other if they get too close when right next to the base. If this occurs, move your last man back a bit. Then move both men forward again.

Steal a base.

Want to get ahead before the ball is hit? Press "STEAL" (Key 7). All your runners move a short distance from their bases. Press the Action Button of the base runner(s) you want to keep going and roll the Speed Roller. If the runner leaves the Base View inset, he cannot return until he appears in full field view. Watch for the pick-off!

Be careful when you press "STEAL." All your runners will have a lead in the full field view even if you don't spin the Speed Roller. You'll have to move quickly if there's a pick-off attempt.

Theme drawing

7

Pages 8, 9, 10, and 11

The topics associated with defense are discussed on these pages.

Page 8 contains another stop-action drawing of a player; and again, this drawing depicts the topic being discussed.

Because the controller options vary from one type of game play to another, the specific functions that are available during each phase of the game are pointed out within the description of the activity. This makes it easier for the user to remember what button will cause a particular action.

DEFENSE (Team In The Field)

PITCHING

You control the type, speed and aim of every pitch. First, press a Keypad Button to set the speed of the pitch (see overlay). Then start the windup and select the pitch type by pressing an Action Button (see overlay). Press the Control Stick as the pitcher winds up to aim the ball high or low, left or right. Here's how you do it:

Drawing shows topic

Pitch Speed:

Select the pitch speed by pressing one of the following Keypad Buttons (see overlay):

Key 1 . . . . Slow pitch

Key 2 . . . . Medium-slow pitch

Key 3 . . . . Medium-fast pitch

Key 4 . . . . Fast pitch

Pitch Type:

Select the pitch type and start the windup by pressing one of the Action Buttons (see overlay):

Yellow . . . . straight pitch

Orange . . . . curve inside

Purple . . . . curve down and outside

Blue . . . . knuckle ball

8

Page 9 contains another screen image. This shows what the screen will look like during play action. Any graphics displayed on the screen which might be confusing to the user are identified on this screen image.

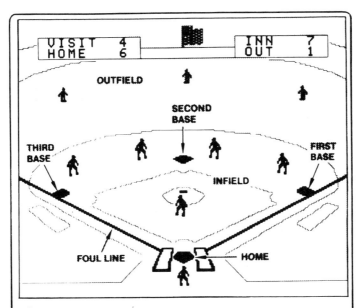

Screen image

Aim:

As the pitcher winds up, you press the Control Stick to adjust the aim of the pitch.

Pressing the Control Stick in **any** direction:

Early . . . . ball tends to go high
Late . . . . ball tends to go low

Pressing the Control Stick:

Left. . . . . .ball tends to go inside
Right. . . . . ball tends to go outside

Combine these two actions for accurate results. For example, press the Control Stick **early** and **left** to make the ball tend to go high and inside.

All good pitchers want to keep the ball low, and now you know how to do it! But remember — once the pitcher releases the ball, pressing the Control Stick has no effect on the pitch.

9

Pages 10 and 11 continue the description of defensive play action. Two more stop-action draw- ings help set the mood and graphically identify the topics being discussed.

Size up your batter.

You can tell after the first couple of pitches what your opponent swings at and what he lets by. Does the batter wait to see what you're going to pitch? Does he take the first pitch that comes along? Pitch him easy if he's not going to swing, then throw him a curve. If he swings at anything, throw him anything. But press your Keypad Buttons out of sight, so he can't see what you're selecting! Be a manager — use your eagle eye and savvy to outwit your opponents. (For Pitching Tips, see page 14.)

FIELDING

Topic drawing

Your fielders can catch, throw or run with the ball! Here's how you do it:

Infield:

When a ball is hit to the infield, move the infielder you want by pressing the Control Stick and the fielder's Action Button (see overlay):

Yellow	First Base
Orange	Second Base
Orange & Purple	Shortstop
Purple	Third Base
Blue	Catcher

10

Be careful in Skill 2 — the ball can bounce off the fielder if he doesn't grab it. Once the fielder has the ball, you don't need to press his Action Button to make him run. Just press the Control Stick in the direction you want him to go! One thing to remember — the pitcher can't tag anyone out.

Throw that ball.

Release the Control Stick and press a base Action Button. Your baseman will meet the ball at the bag. If the second baseman fields the ball, the shortstop will cover second when you throw. Don't worry about his ability. Your players throw perfectly every time!

Outfield:

When a hit clears the infield, the outfielders become the active, controlled players. Move the outfielder you want by pressing the Control Stick and the outfielder's Action Button (see overlay):

Topic drawing

Yellow . . . . Right Field
Orange . . . . Center Field
Purple . . . . Left Field

Home!

Once the fielder has the ball, you don't need to press his Action Button. To make him run, press the Control Stick in the direction you want him to go. To throw the ball to the infield, release the Control Stick and press the base Action Button. Remember — your fielder throws to a base, not to a man. When the play is over, press "RETURN" (Key #). The ball automatically returns to the pitcher.

11

Pages 12, 13, 14, and 15

Page 12 has a short paragraph at the top of the page that tells the user how the game is won and how a winner is determined.

Page 13 has a similar paragraph at the top that describes scoring. By putting this paragraph across from the one on page 12, the reader can quickly find scoring and winning information.

How to win

It ain't over till it's over!

The score's tied at the bottom of the ninth. Your last man is up. He strikes out. The game's not over yet! HEAD-TO-HEAD™ BASEBALL lasts for as many innings as it takes to establish a winner. However, if the home team is winning after the visitor's third out in the ninth inning, the game stops and home wins.

TRAINING

Unhappy with your performance?

Try some training. Just for starters, hit one of the Fielding Game Options and play a few rounds. That's the best way to get your players used to picking up the ball and throwing to **any** base. That's important, because you don't always want to throw to first in a game. Your out should be the lead base runner, because he'll try to score first.

Double Plays

There aren't any base runners in field training, but you can still practice throwing to second and then to first as fast as you can. Speed and accuracy are the keys to any successful double play. How quickly can you pick up that ball? How soon can the second baseman heave it to first? Work, work, work! It'll pay off in the game.

Pick off.

If a runner leaves his base inset during the lead off, you stand a good chance of picking him off. Press "PICK-OFF" (Key 9). If the windup has not started, the view changes to full field, and your pitcher throws to the base you select. If the windup **has** started, the pitch is thrown, then the catcher makes the pick-off play. The pitcher cannot balk!

12

The next topic that's discussed is game play techniques. The manual provides pointers and suggestions to help the game player improve his skills. Notice that the tips are limited and suggest steps the user might take to practice his playing skills. Part of the fun of playing a game is to discover new ways to enjoy the game as well as short cuts that aren't documented in the instruction

Scoring.

Runners who cross home plate score one run. But if the ball is caught, and the runner on third didn't tag up, his run will not count. If the ball is thrown to third before the runner tags up, he is out. And, if the third out is made on a force play, runs do not score, just as in professional baseball.

How to win

Reset.

The Reset Button on the console stops the game and returns you to the Title Screen. It can be used to start a new game at any time, and can also be used in the event of game malfunction.

How to end game

BATTING TIPS

You start your swing when you press the Control Stick. The direction you press the Control Stick is the direction you'll swing your bat.

Topic drawing

13

booklet. This idea is reinforced on page 15 in the section entitled THE FUN OF DISCOVERY.

As a programmer, you probably know all the sneaky, devious ways to short-cut game play. After all, you programmed the game to work the ways you wanted it to. Don't spoil the excitement for your user. There's a fine line between telling too much and not telling enough. Your user needs to know

Hints on improving your batting

In games played at Skill 1, it's pretty easy to connect with the ball. In games played at Skill 2, watch the following:

1. Hit the ball right on and it will fly straight out. (You might even get a homer!)
2. Swing under the ball and it will tend to go higher.
3. Swing over the ball and it will tend to be a grounder.
4. Hit the ball inside and it will tend to go right.
5. Hit the ball outside and it will tend to go left.
6. Hit the ball early and it will tend to go left.
7. Hit the ball late and it will tend to go right.

PITCHING TIPS

The only way to pitch your best is to practice! Try timing your release of the ball by pressing the Control Stick in the middle of your windup. Then release the ball earlier or later and watch how the ball goes higher or lower across the plate. Experiment with each type of pitch. See what happens

14

enough to successfully play the game on at least an elementary level. You can even provide hints on how the user can move on to more sophisticated game play. Just don't let the user in on all the special features you've put into the game. If for no other reason, you want to be able to beat any opponents that want to challenge you, the creator!

when you bring the pitch inside or outside — especially on those tricky curve balls!

It's possible to throw into the strike zone with every type of pitch. Practice with the Control Stick to perfect your aim. Try some of the following:

1. Mix the types and speeds of pitches you throw. Don't fall into the same pattern pitch after pitch. (But see tips 3 and 4 below.)

2. Don't always throw strikes. Keep the batter guessing. If he's expecting a ball, throw a strike. Likewise, if he's looking toward the strike zone, throw a ball.

3. Adjust your pitches to the batter. Some batters will fall for the same type of pitch each time.

4. If you want to throw the same type of pitch twice in a row, vary the second pitch by changing its speed or throwing in a different direction.

5. Adjust your pitch to the count. If the batter's count is 3 balls and no strikes, pitch to the strike zone.

6. If the batter is outguessing you, try a knuckle ball. But be careful — knuckle balls often miss the strike zone.

Hints on improving your pitching

THE FUN OF DISCOVERY

This instruction booklet will provide the basic information you need to get started playing SUPER ACTION™ BASEBALL, but it is only the beginning! You will find that this cartridge is full of special features that make SUPER ACTION™ BASE-BALL exciting every time you play. Experiment with different techniques — and enjoy the game!

15

Pages 16, 17, and 18

These pages deal with some marketing and responsibility topics. If you're sharing your game with a limited audience, you probably won't have to worry about replacing disks, tapes, or joystick overlays. You also won't need to be too concerned with warranty and service policy information. If you market your game through a publisher, the publishing company will handle the details. They will outline any ongoing responsibilities on your part in

---

**REPLACEMENT OVERLAYS FOR
SUPER ACTION™ BASEBALL #2423**

If accessories, such as Keypad Overlay Sets used with some games only, are not available at your local dealer, they can be ordered from Coleco Industries, Inc. directly. Information can be obtained on how to order from Coleco's toll-free hotline: 1-800-842-1225 nationwide. This service is in operation from 8:00 a.m. to 5:00 p.m. Eastern Standard Time, Monday through Friday.

Overlay Set . . . . No. 91987 (2 per set)

16

your contract. Typically, these might include fixing any bugs that are found or making other coding changes that are required.

When you decide to market a game or other type of program to the general public, replacement parts, warranties, and service contracts are your responsibility. You need to tell your customers what they can expect from you if they have problems running your program, if they receive a damaged tape or disk, or if they ruin something.

90-DAY LIMITED WARRANTY

Coleco warrants to the original consumer purchaser in the United States of America that this video game cartridge will be free of defects in material or workmanship for 90 days from the date of purchase under normal in-house use.

Coleco's sole and exclusive liability for defects in material and workmanship shall be limited to repair or replacement at its authorized Coleco Service Station. This warranty does not obligate Coleco to bear the cost of transportation charges in connection with the repair or replacement of defective parts.

This warranty is invalid if the damage or defect is caused by accident, act of God, consumer abuse, unauthorized alteration or repair, vandalism, or misuse.

Any implied warranties arising out of the sale of the video game cartridges including the implied warranties of merchantability and fitness for a particular purpose are limited to the above 90 day period. Coleco shall in no event be liable for incidental, consequential, contingent or any other damages.

This warranty gives you specific legal rights, and you may have other rights which vary from State to State. Some states do not allow the exclusion or limitation of incidental or consequential damages or limitations on how long an implied warranty lasts, so the above limitations or exclusions may not apply to you.

SERVICE POLICY

Please read your Video Game Owner's Manual carefully before using the product. If your video game cartridge fails to operate properly, please refer to the trouble-shooting checklist in the Owner's Manual for your particular video system. If you cannot correct the malfunction after consulting the trouble-shooting checklist, please call Customer Service on

17

Warranty info— your protection

151

Take a look at the language that is used in these sections of the booklet. You'll get an idea as to what problems you need to address when you get ready to mass market your programs. Before you jump in and write your own text, you may want to consult with an attorney who specializes in this type of writing. He can help you prepare a document that you can include with your program. He may even be able to help write a *boilerplate* document that you can use with all your programs.

Coleco's toll-free service hotline: 1-800-842-1225 nationwide. This service is in operation from 8:00 a.m. to 5:00 p.m. Eastern Standard Time, Monday through Friday.

If Customer Service advises you to return your video game cartridge, please return it postage prepaid and insured, with your name, address, proof of the date of purchase, and a brief description of the problem to the Service Station you have been directed to return it to by the toll-free service information. If your cartridge is found to be factory defective during the first 90 days, it will be repaired or replaced at no cost to you. If the cartridge is found to have been consumer damaged or abused and therefore not covered by the warranty, then you will be advised, in advance, of repair costs.

If your cartridge requires service after expiration of the 90 day Limited Warranty period, please call Coleco's toll-free service hotline for instructions on how to proceed: 1-800-842-1225 nationwide.

18

Pages 19 and 20

These two pages contain the copyright and trademark information for the game. Notice the way in which the information is presented, and the parts of the game that are trademarked instead of copyrighted.

SUPER ACTION™, HEAD-TO-HEAD™ and ADAM™ are trademarks of Coleco Industries, Inc.

ColecoVision® is a trademark of Coleco Industries, Inc. for its game system, expansion modules, and cartridges.

Package, Program and Audiovisual © 1983 Coleco Industries, Inc. Amsterdam, New York 12010

The copyright notice

19

In this booklet, the editor decided to put this information on a separate page at the back. You may want to include this information on one of the first pages in your manual.

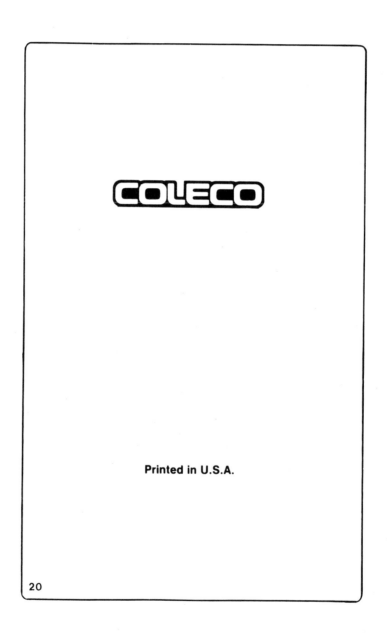

COLECO

Printed in U.S.A.

20

Appendix B

The Invoice Entry Program

This appendix takes a single program called Invoice Entry and shows how it can be documented using the formats described in the text. The program is part of an accounts payable system. As you read through this appendix, you will find many types of documentation that you could use to describe a program that you are writing or have written. Each sample is preceded by an explanation of what it is. This explanation describes both the format and the way the format was applied to the specific program. The following is a list of the documentation samples you will find in this appendix.

DFD

Annotated Listing
Block Diagram
~~Chapin Chart~~
Data Dictionary
File Description list struct
~~Flowchart~~ organigramme
Logic List
Problem Statement
Program Listing
Program Narrative
Pseudocode
Reference Manual
Sample Report
Screen Image
Self-Study Guide
Specifications
Step-by-Step Instructions

The samples have been arranged in alphabetical order according to type. This is not necessarily the order in which you would arrange them if you were including them in a documentation manual.

ANNOTATED LISTING

There are many ways to use an annotated listing. During development coding, you can print a listing of your code and use it to identify problem lines and problem subroutines. If you're having trouble getting the code to do what you want it to do, you may want to print a listing and note the trouble spots; then take a break. When you return to work on your program, your annotated listing will remind you of the code lines you need to work on.

When your program is finished and working correctly, you can make handwritten notations on the printed code listing to highlight special subroutines that you could reuse in other programs. Your handwritten notations can also help you as you write a program narrative. Instead of rereading the code, you can scan your notes and pick out the detailed information you need to explain how the program works.

You can also put notes into lines of code in your program. The lines with notes are called comment lines. Each system has different rules for how to code comment lines. In this system, the word REM is used to identify a REMinder or comment line. The comment lines for this invoice entry program, which is shown in Fig. B-1, are lines 230, 380, 470, and 540.

In this program, the comment lines explain how the program should work and where various processing steps take place in the code. The handwritten comments show where the program is not working and which lines of code need correcting.

```
 40  DIM a$(256)
 70  PRINT "What is the invoice date?";
 80  INPUT da$
 90  PRINT: PRINT "What is the Vendor's Name?";
100  INPUT v$: v$ = LEFT$(v$, 7)
105  IF v$ = "" THEN 90
110  PRINT
120  PRINT "Enter the item amounts"
130  PRINT "one at a time. Enter"; CHR$(34); "O"; CHR$(34);
     " as an"
140  PRINT "amount when done."
150  PRINT
160  PRINT v$; " INVOICE, "; da$
170  PRINT "_____"
180  n = n+1
190  PRINT "Item #"; n; ":";
200  INPUT a$(n)
210  IF a$(n) = "O" THEN 230
220  GOTO 180
230  REM     total the entries
240  FOR x = 1 TO n
250  t = t+VAL(a$(x))
260  NEXT x
270  PRINT
280  PRINT "These items total to $"; t
290  PRINT
300  PRINT "Does this match the printed copy?"
310  INPUT m$
320  IF LEFT$(m$, 1) <> "Y" AND LEFT$(m$, 1) <> "y" THEN 540
340  PRINT "Everything checks out..."
350  PRINT
360  PRINT "one moment while the items and total"
370  PRINT "are filed for storage"
380  REM     file values into ".dp"
390  v$ = v$+".dp"
400  PRINT CHR$(4); "open "; v$: PRINT CHR$(4); "close "; v$
410  PRINT CHR$(4); "append "; v$
420  FOR x = 1 TO n-1
430  PRINT a$(x)
440  NEXT x
```

Items + amounts entered one at a time.

Not totaling after corrected values are entered

Not filing properly

```
450 PRINT STR$(t)
460 PRINT CHR$(4); "close "; v$
470 REM      all done!
480 HOME
510 PRINT: PRINT "Invoice checking complete..."
520 PRINT: PRINT "Have a Nice Day"
530 PRINT: PRINT: END
540 REM       verify & correct
550 PRINT
560 PRINT "Let's check the amounts..."
570 PRINT
580 PRINT "item", "amount"
590 PRINT "_____"
600 FOR x = 1 TO n-1
610 PRINT x, a$(x)
620 PRINT "OK (Y/N?)";
630 INPUT ac$
640 IF LEFT$(ac$, 1) <> "Y" AND LEFT$(ac$, 1) <> "y" THEN
GOTO 670
650 NEXT x
660 t = 0: FOR x = 1 TO n-1: t = t = VAL(a$(x)):  NEXT x:
GOTO 270
670 PRINT "Enter corrected value";
680 INPUT a$(x)
690 GOTO 610
```

N or any other response defaults to No. ←

Fig. B-1. Annotated listing: invoice entry program.

BLOCK DIAGRAM

A block diagram shows high-level relationships between programs within a system or subroutines within a program. It provides a quick graphic overview of the processing.

The block diagram for the accounts payable system, shown in Fig. B-2, shows how all of the programs work together to get the job of paying bills accomplished. The drawing suggests an interface between the accounts payable system and a general ledger system.

None of the actual processing logic is shown in this high-level diagram. The primary input is invoice information. Several files are updated after processing has taken place. These include the general ledger file, the vendor file, and the checking account file. The primary output from the accounts payable system is the checks for the vendors. In addition, a variety of reports are available. Some of these provide information that can be used to check input and processing for accuracy. The invoice register and the check preview register are examples of this kind of printout. Other reports provide information that can be used for analysis and kept on

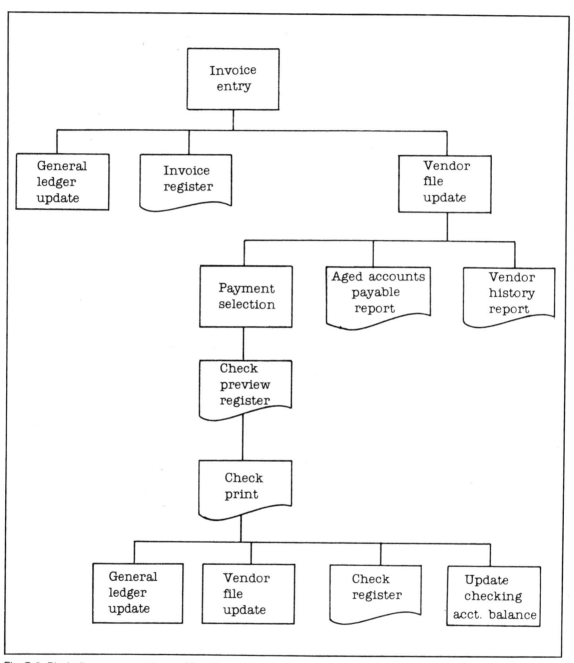

Fig. B-2. Block diagram: accounts payable program.

file. The aged accounts payable report, vendor history report, and check register are examples of this kind of printout.

Each of the boxes on this diagram represents multiple processing steps. If these steps were included in detail, the block diagram would become too complicated to be meaningful. It would also provide users with more information than they need in a high-level overview chart.

CHAPIN CHART

When you begin to design the processing logic required for your program, you may find it helpful to prepare a chart showing the processing steps, iterations, and decisions. There are several ways to chart the logic of your program. If you like to work vertically and use lined notebook-style paper, the Chapin chart may offer the best format for you.

This Chapin chart, shown in Fig. B-3, shows the logic flow for the invoice entry program. The processing begins when the user enters an invoice date. This date is processed through a validation routine. The details of the routine are omitted from this chart because they are an independent miniprogram or subroutine. This validation subroutine could be shared or called by several programs within the accounts payable system.

If the date passes the validation test, the user can enter a vendor ID. This entry is also passed through a validation subroutine. Again, the details of the subroutine are not shown on this chart. Like the date validation, the vendor ID validation could be shared or called by many different programs within the accounts payable system.

The next step in the processing is the entry of line item amounts. The user enters the amounts one by one. As the amounts are entered, they are accumulated. When the user enters a zero, the program is signaled that there are no more amounts to enter for the invoice.

When all of the line item amounts have been entered, the program prints the total amount it has accumulated. The program asks the user to check the total against the total on the printed invoice from the vendor. If the two don't match, the program begins a correction subroutine. The details of this subroutine have been omitted from this chart. If the two totals match, the program lets the user begin entering the next invoice record.

The final processing steps in the program write information to the vendor file, the general ledger file, and the invoice register report. The detailed processing for these information transfer routines is omitted from this chart.

This program contains two loops. The major loop allows the user to enter many invoices before transferring the information from these invoices. The minor loop lets the user enter many item amounts for each invoice.

As you can see, this Chapin chart shows detailed processing information for the invoice entry program. The details for several of the subroutines that are included in this program are omitted. This is because these subroutines are like miniprograms. Including their detailed processing logic would clutter and distract from the critical path of the invoice entry program. Each of these subroutines should be diagrammed with a chart of its own.

DATA DICTIONARY

This dictionary, shown in Fig. B-4, provides definitions of terms found in the accounts payable system. The definitions are system specific.

FILE DESCRIPTIONS

Figure B-5 shows the file descriptions for three of the primary files maintained by the accounts payable system. Other files are created during processing, but in many cases, these are temporary files, which disappear after the processing is completed. The invoice register creates

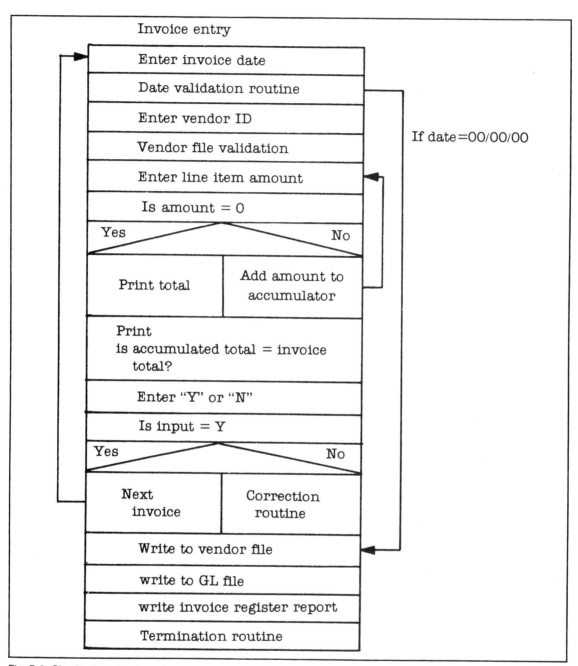

Fig. B-3. Chapin chart: invoice entry program.

ACCOUNTS PAYABLE

A system that records invoice amounts due vendors and generates payment checks for these amounts. The system also keeps detailed vendor records and payment records. Information that is input or derived from the processing in the programs within this system is transferred to other files within the BSI office automation system if the appropriate interface switches have been initialized.

AGED ACCOUNTS PAYABLE REPORTS

A printed report that shows the balance amounts due to vendors. These amounts are divided into four categories: current, over 30, over 60, and over 90. An accumulated balance for each vendor is also shown. Totals information showing the total amount due all vendors (currently, over 30, over 60, and over 90) is printed along with a grand total showing outstanding obligations.

CHECK

A printed document issuing payment to a vendor. Checks are printed automatically and can cover multiple invoice amounts.

CHECK PREVIEW REGISTER

A printed report that shows the checks that will be printed, their individual amounts, and the total amount based on the payment selections that are made by the user. As the name suggests, this is a preview document. No checks are printed when this report is printed, and no files are updated. The user has the opportunity to review the impact of his payment selections and then proceed with check printing or cancel the printing and reselect the payments to be made.

CHECK PRINT

A program that prints checks issuing payment to vendors. In addition to printing the actual checks, this program also transfers update information to the general ledger file, the vendor file, and the checking account file. The detail and summary information for the checks that are printed is reported in the check register report. This report is automatically prepared as the checks are printed.

CHECK REGISTER

A printed report showing detail and summary information for a batch of vendor payment checks.

CHECKING ACCOUNT FILE

A file that maintains the balance amount in the checking account from which vendor payment checks are drawn. As deposits are made, the balance increases. Before payment selection is approved, the balance is checked to be sure there are sufficient funds in the account to cover the total amount of the vendor checks being issued.

Fig. B-4. Data dictionary: invoice entry program.

INVOICE

A printed document issued by a vendor detailing purchases and corresponding amounts.

INVOICE DATE

The date on which the vendor issued the invoice. It is not the date on which the invoice was received. The date is used as a reference index for invoices. If a dispute arises, both your company and the vendor will have a common reference point.

INVOICE ENTRY

A program that lets the user enter detailed information from vendor invoices. This program then selectively distributes the information throughout the system.

INVOICE REGISTER

A printed report that shows the detail and summary information for a batch of invoices. This report is generated automatically after the last invoice in a batch has been entered.

VENDOR FILE

A file in which detailed information on vendors is maintained.

VENDOR HISTORY REPORT

A printed report showing the invoices, payments, and total amount spent with a given vendor during a fiscal year. The report can be printed at any time and will reflect the most up-to-date yearly amounts. The records on this report are sorted alphabetically by vendor ID and then subsorted by date.

VENDOR ID

A unique identification code assigned to each vendor. The code may be up to 7 characters in length and may contain both letters and numbers.

Fig. B-4. Continued.

such a temporary file. After the register is printed, the print file that collected the information for printing is deleted. The information that appears on the register is saved in the vendor file and the vendor history file.

More information is stored in some files than may be readily apparent to the user. The operator who enters the invoice amounts into the accounts payable system works only with the vendor ID field from the vendor file. The other information that is kept the vendor file is not needed for the invoice entry program, so it is not presented nor made available to the operator.

The operator entering invoice information is also not aware that his initials as well as the date and time of the entry are recorded. This information is kept in the invoice file so that it can be retrieved and analyzed if needed.

The file descriptions provide useful technical information to users. It shows them where to look

Invoice File:

Invoice Date:	MM/DD/YY
Line Item Amount	999.999.99
Total Amount	9.999.999.99
Vendor ID	6 characters A/N
Operator Initials	3 characters A/N
Date of Entry	MM/DD/YY
Time of Entry	00:00:00

Vendor File

Vendor ID	6 characters A/N
Vendor Name	25 characters A/N
Vendor Address	30 characters A/N
Vendor City	25 characters A/N
Vendor State	2 characters A/N
Vendor Zip Code	9 characters A/N
Current Balance	999.999.99
Over 30	999.999.99
Over 60	999.999.99
Over 90	999.999.99
Total Balance	9.999.999.99

Vendor History File

Vendor ID	6 characters A/N
Invoice Date	MM/DD/YY
Line Item Amount	999.999.99
Total Amount Due	9.999.999.99
YTD Total Due	9.999.999.99
Payment Date	MM/DD/YY
Check No.	99999
Check Amount	99.999.99
YTD Total Paid	9.999.999.99

Fig. B-5. File description: invoice entry program.

for various items and how to understand the sizes and data requirements for the fields. This information is important to any user who must make custom modifications to the system.

Many times, a user needs to write special report programs to meet special needs. File descriptions show the user where field data is stored and the format in which it is kept. The user then knows which files to include in his report and what must be done to the field data to get the report to show the information he needs.

FLOWCHART

A flowchart is a method for graphically representing the processing logic of a program. Special symbols are used to depict different types of processing. The flowchart can be drawn vertically and horizontally. In Fig. B-6, the flowchart was drawn vertically so that it would comfortably fit on a single page.

The program begins with the user entering an invoice date. Because the date is entered manually by the user, the manual entry symbol is used.

The date is then validated by the date validation routine. This routine is depicted with a process symbol. The complete details of the validation process are omitted from this flowchart.

If the date passes the validation check, the user must enter the vendor ID. Again, this is manual input, so the appropriate symbol is used. The vendor ID is validated by the vendor file validation routine. Like the date validation routine, this is depicted with a process symbol and details are omitted.

If the vendor validation is successful, the user can enter the first line amount. This amount is checked and a processing decision is made. The horizontal diamond shape indicates a processing decision.

If the line amount entered is not equal to zero, the program takes the amount that was entered and adds it to an accumulator. The user is then permitted to enter the next line amount. This processing cycle continues until the line amount is tested and determined to be zero. Sometimes called a loop, this iterative processing is depicted with arrows that indicate the processing steps that are included in the cycle.

When the line amount is zero, the loop or iteration is broken. The processing then "falls through" to the next step. The amount from the accumulator is displayed and the user is asked to determine whether the amount being displayed is equal to the amount printed on the vendor's invoice.

If the amounts are not equal, the program begins a correction routine. The details of the processing are not displayed in this chart. The correction routine takes the processing back to the point where the total amount in the accumulator is printed. The user is then asked to determine whether the accumulated amount and the invoice amounts are equal. Each time the user types N, the correction routine is called. This loop or iteration continues until the user is able to obtain a match.

After a match is achieved, the processing falls through to the next processing operation.

Information collected in this program is passed to the general ledger system and the vendor file. These updates take place automatically and involve files within the system. For this reason, the input/output symbol is used to indicate the data transfer.

At the same time the files are updated, an invoice register report is prepared. The details of both the update processing and the report preparation are omitted from this flowchart.

When the updates and report processing are complete, the program is ready to accept the next invoice entry. This giant loop or iteration is the primary processing cycle for the program. It continues until a date of 00/00/00 is entered. The date validation subroutine tests for this date, and when it is encountered, the validation routine sends the processing directly to the termination routine.

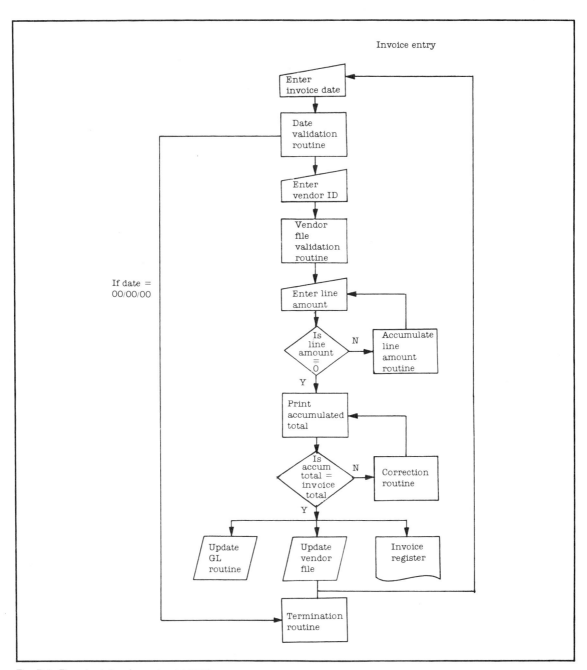

Invoice entry

Enter invoice date

Date validation routine

If date = 00/00/00

Enter vendor ID

Vendor file validation routine

Enter line amount

Is line amount = 0
N → Accumulate line amount routine

Y

Print accumulated total

Is accum total = invoice total
N → Correction routine

Y

Update GL routine

Update vendor file

Invoice register

Termination routine

Fig. B-6. Flowchart: invoice entry program.

```
Input invoice date as reference number.
Input vendor ID
Input line item amounts
Total line items amounts
Verify total against total on invoice.

If totals don't match. allow corrections.

Update general ledger accounts
Update vendor file
Print invoice register report
```

Fig. B-7. Logic list: invoice entry program.

for two reasons. First, it reduces the clutter on the flowchart and streamlines the graphic elements if only the items that directly impact the critical path of the logic are included. Second, the decisions and other processing steps that take place within the subroutines are important to the critical path of those subroutines, but they are only tangential to the critical path of the program being charted. If all of the processing details were included for all of the subroutines, the user would be distracted and might misinterpret the critical path of the logic for the pimary program.

LOGIC LIST

A logic list is like a shopping list. A shopping list tells you what groceries you need to get, but it doesn't say how much to buy or which brands to get. A logic list tells you what processing steps you need, but it doesn't tell you how many subroutines you'll need or how you should code the logic.

The logic list helps you think through the processing you'll need to code. Some people find it easier to work with logic lists than with flowcharts or Chapin charts. A logic list is usually written during the development phase of a program. From the logic list, you can prepare pseudocode or detailed flowcharts for each processing subroutine you'll need to code. The logic list for the invoice entry program is shown in Fig. B-7.

The termination process zeros all accumulators, clears out all field data, and deletes any temporary files that have been created. It then returns the user to the main menu for the accounts payable system. The details of this termination processing are omitted from this flowchart.

Looking at the flowchart, it's easy to find the three loops in the program. The information that must be typed in by the user is easy to locate. Because of the symbols that are used, the user can quickly determine the kinds of processing that take place in the program. Subroutine logic is summarized in process blocks. This technique is used

The invoice entry program allows line amounts and invoice totals to be transferred from the hardcopy vendor invoices into the system and to be distributed to the appropriate files. The vendor ID and the invoice date must be recorded along with the individual item amounts and the total amount. The detail information for each batch of invoices is to be printed on an invoice register. The total dollar amounts for each invoice must be conveyed to the vendor file and the general ledger file.

Fig. B-8. Problem statement: invoice entry program.

PROBLEM STATEMENT

The problem statement identifies the primary objective of the program. In the case of the invoice entry program, the primary objective is to get the dollar figures from the printed vendor invoices into the system.

As shown in Fig. B-8, the problem statement also details some of the tasks the program will perform. In this case, the program will record the invoice date, vendor ID, line amounts, and total amount. The program will also pass portions of this information to two files and one report.

The problem statement tells you, in a nutshell, what purpose each program has and why it is being included in a system. A problem statement can also be written for each subroutine within a program. In this case, the statement would explain what the function of the subroutine was and why it was an essential part of the program. In most cases, programmers don't write problem statements for individual subroutines. This is only done when a subroutine is very complicated, or when it is shared (called) by many different programs within the system. The date validation subroutine might warrant a problem statement because it is used by many programs within the accounts payable system.

If the program has lots of restrictions or must deal with tricky exception situations, you should mention these in the problem statement.

The problem statement should be kept short. It's designed to be a summary statement that concisely describes the purpose of the program or subroutine. Detailed processing information the programmer will need in order to design code should be put in the program specification rather than in the problem statement.

Many times, the program designer will preface a program specification document with a problem statement. This reveals to the programmer the big picture of what the program is supposed to do, before he wades through the detailed logic requirements.

PROGRAM LISTING

A program listing is simply a printout of the code for a program.

Your code listing provides a detailed roadmap to the logic of your program. Good roadmaps provide landmarks to help the driver get from one place to another easily and with a minimum amount of guesswork and frustration. Your comment statements provide landmarks for anyone trying to read your code.

The first landmark that's needed is the starting point. In the case of your program, the first landmark you provide is the comment narrative that precedes the first line of actual code. This comment narrative gives you the name of the program, the date it was written, and the author (in most cases, you). It also shows the dates modifications were made to the program.

If you sprinkle comment statements throughout your code, other programmers will be able to read the code more easily. It's important to call attention to your comment statements. Many professional programmers emphasize their comment statements by putting a string of asterisks before and after them. In long, complicated programs, the subroutines are usually named, and the names are enclosed in a box made of asterisks. If you look at the listing for the invoice entry program shown in Fig. B-9, you can see how the comment statements have been highlighted with asterisks.

PROGRAM NARRATIVE

The program narrative serves many functions. It introduces the user to the program and provides a general overview as to what the program does and how it works. It's also an excellent place to include preliminary set-up instructions.

In the example shown in Fig. B-10, the program narrative is divided into four sections. If you are documenting a system with many programs, you may want to present each of the four topics in

```
  5 REM   *******************************
 10 REM   * INVOICE ENTRY PROGRAM        *
 20 REM   * BSI ACCOUNTS PAYABLE SYSTEM*
 30 REM   * John Pellino, January 1984 *
 35 REM   *******************************
 40 DIM a$(256)
 70 PRINT "What is the invoice date?";
 80 INPUT da$
 90 PRINT: PRINT "What is the Vendor's Name?";
100 INPUT v$: v$ = LEFT$(v$, 7)
105 IF v$ = "" THEN 90
110 PRINT
120 PRINT "Enter the item amounts"
130 PRINT "one at a time. Enter"; CHR$(34); "0"; CHR$(34);
" as an"
140 PRINT "amount when done."
150 PRINT
160 PRINT v$; " INVOICE, "; da$
170 PRINT "_____"
180 n = n+1
190 PRINT "Item #"; n; ":";
200 INPUT a$(n)
210 IF a$(n) = "0" THEN 230
220 GOTO 180
230 REM   *******TOTAL THE ENTRIES *******
240 FOR x = 1 TO n
250 t = t+VAL(a$(x))
260 NEXT x
270 PRINT
280 PRINT "These items total to $"; t
290 PRINT
300 PRINT "Does this match the printed copy?"
310 INPUT m$
320 IF LEFT$(m$, 1) <> "Y" AND LEFT$(m$, 1) <> "y" THEN 540
340 PRINT "Everything checks out..."
350 PRINT
360 PRINT "one moment while the items and total"
370 PRINT "are filed for storage"
380 REM   ******* FILE VALUES INTO ".dp" *******
390 v$ = v$+".dp"
```

```
400 PRINT CHR$(4); "open "; v$: PRINT CHR$(4); "close "; v$
410 PRINT CHR$(4); "append "; v$
420 FOR x = 1 TO n-1
430 PRINT a$(x)
440 NEXT x
450 PRINT STR$(t)
460 PRINT CHR$(4); "close "; v$
470 REM  ****** ALL DONE ... HOORAY ******
480 HOME
510 PRINT: PRINT "Invoice checking complete..."
520 PRINT: PRINT "Have a Nice Day"
530 PRINT: PRINT: END
540 REM  ****** VERIFY AND CORRECT ******
550 PRINT
560 PRINT "Let's check the amounts..."
570 PRINT
580 PRINT "item", "amount"
590 PRINT "_____        "
600 FOR x = 1 TO n-1
610 PRINT x, a$(x)
620 PRINT "OK (Y/N?)";
630 INPUT ac$
640 IF LEFT$(ac$, 1) <> "Y" AND LEFT$(ac$, 1) <> "y" THEN
GOTO 670
650 NEXT x
660 t = 0: FOR x = 1 TO n-1: t = t = VAL(a$(x)): NEXT x:
GOTO 270
670 PRINT "Enter corrected value";
680 INPUT a$(x)
690 GOTO 610
```

Fig. B-9. Program listing: invoice entry program.

this narrative as a separate section of your documentation. If you do this, most of your programs would be included four times, once for each section. If you're only providing one program, you can include all the topics within the program narrative.

The first section of this narrative provides an introduction to the program. Because this is a business program, the introduction is aimed at the supervisors and management personnel who will be working with the system. It describes the general capabilities of the program and tells how it fits into the overall system.

The first section also alerts management to the preparation work that must be done before the pro-

Introduction

The invoice entry program is the first program that is run during the daily operations of the accounts payable system. This is the program that transfers the information from the printed invoices you receive from the vendor to the system. Once this information is entered, the system can provide you with the data you need to decide what checks to print.

Before this program can be run, you must run the vendor maintenance program and assign vendor IDs to your vendors. When a vendor ID is entered as part of an invoice, the ID is checked against the vendor file to be sure that no typographical error has been made.

You will also need to run the start of day program before entering invoices. This provides the system with the information it needs to record the date and time each invoice was entered.

The invoice entry program has been designed to speed up the entry of invoice information. Invoices can be entered in any order. Simply collect a batch of invoices, and enter the information requested by the program. Because the invoices are identified by date and vendor ID, they can be entered at any time during the month. Payment selection is based on all invoices that have been entered into the system.

This design lets accounts-payable staff enter invoices into the system as time permits. Rather than collecting the invoices for a month and entering them in one large batch, the data entry task can be divided into shorter sessions. This reduces the fatigue factor on the part of the staff and minimizes the chances for errors.

Program Overview

The invoice entry program prompts you to enter the specific pieces of information from each vendor invoice you receive. The vendor ID and the invoice date are used to uniquely identify each invoice. Duplicate IDs and dates are permitted so that if you receive more than one invoice from a vendor that is dated with the same date, the system will not reject it.

The individual line-item amounts must be recorded. These are printed on the invoice register report and should be saved for historical reference. As these amounts are entered, the system automatically adds them together and determines a total dollar amount for the invoice. When the last line-item amount has been entered, the system prints the total amount it has calculated. The operator must check this amount against the amount printed on the vendor invoice. If the two amounts match, the system gets ready to accept the next invoice entry.

If the amounts don't match, your operator is given the opportunity to review the line item amounts. The amount values can be corrected, duplicated entries can be deleted, and skipped entries can be added.

When all of the invoices in the batch have been entered, the system exists from this program and returns to the main menu.

The system automatically produces an invoice register so that a permanent and detailed record of the invoices can be kept on file. In addition, the system automatically updates the vendor file with the newly entered amounts.

Installation

This program is installed automatically when the accounts payable system is loaded. If you have purchased the BSI General Ledger system and want to have invoice information automatically passed to the appropriate general ledger accounts, you will need to activate the interface between the two systems.

To activate the interface, you need to begin at the main menu for the accounts payable system. In the blank area where you would normally type your program selection, type: IE-GL, then press the RETURN key.

A question will appear on the screen asking you, "Do you want to activate the invoice entry to general ledger interface?" Type the word YES; then press the RETURN key.

The message "Interface being activated." will appear on your screen. A few moments later, the message "Interface completed." will appear on the screen, and the system will automatically return to the main menu of the accounts payable system.

If the interface has already been activated, you will see the message "Interface already activated." instead of the "Interface complete" message.

If the interface cannot be activated (that is, if you don't have the general ledger system),the message "NOT A VALID SELECTION" will appear when you type the program name and press the RETURN key.

Checkout Procedure

To be sure your invoice entry program is working properly, you can run the following tests. These can be run at any time.

Test 1

1. Choose the invoice entry program from the main menu.

Fig. B-10. Program narrative: invoice entry program.

2. Type 00/00/00 when the program asks you for the date.
3. The message "Batch complete" should appear on the screen and you should be returned to the main menu screen.

Test 2

1. Choose the invoice entry program from the main menu.
2. Type in the date 06/99/87.
3. The message "Invalid date" should appear.

Test 3

1. Choose the invoice entry program from the main menu.
2. Type in a valid date.
3. Type XXXX as the vendor ID.
4. The message "No such vendor on file" should appear.

Test 4

1. Choose the invoice entry program from the main menu.
2. Type in a valid date.
3. Type TEST as the vendor ID.
4. Type in the following line item amounts:
   10.00
   20.00
   30.00
   40.00
   00.00
5. The total amount should be 100.00

If any of the tests do not produce the results indicated, check your entries. If they seem correct, try running the test again. If the results are still incorrect, call your BSI technical representative. Tell the representative which test you were running, and what your results were.

Fig. B-10. Continued.

gram can be run successfully.

Because management and supervisory personnel can be tough customers, the benefits of using the automated approach are stressed through-

out the introduction. Part of the purpose of the introduction to this program is to get management to endorse and support the program.

The second topic covered in the narrative is

the overview. This section provides a high-level explanation of the processing that takes place within the program.

Again, this section is addressed to managers and supervisors. It can also be read by operators, however, to give them a general idea of what the program does.

The third section deals with installing the program. Because the program is part of a larger system, the only instruction that's included in this section is the access to the interface switch.

If you're providing a single program, you'll need to expand this section to tell the user how to load the program into his system. He'll also need to know how to modify the program to work with the configuration he has. For example, some popular word processing programs that are designed to work on many systems have special installation programs that automatically "fix" them so they work on the user's computer system. These word processing programs also offer a printer option program that lets the user get his printer hooked into the system properly.

The last section of this narrative is a checkout procedure for the program. This lets the user perform a series of tests to test whether or not the program is working properly. The tests are specially designed to pinpoint which areas of the program are not working correctly. The user doesn't need to know any coding or programming to perform the tests; but the results he gets will quickly tell a programmer or technical representative which parts of the code have problems.

As you may have guessed from the test input, certain test data has been provided with this program. This data was built into the code so that the user could run the tests easily.

The tests that are shown for this program are the kinds of tests you should run when you're checking your program code. If you keep detailed records when you test your program, you'll have no trouble providing your user with examples to use when he checks out the program.

Providing your user with checkout tests serves two purposes. First, it reassures him that the program is working properly. Second, it shows him how the program will respond to specific types of data.

As mentioned earlier, you may decide to make some of the topics included in this program narrative into separate sections. The two topics which are most commonly given their own sections are the installation procedures and the checkout tests.

PSEUDOCODE

Pseudocode lets you work through the logic of a program without worrying about coding syntax. This quasi-code is written using code-like phrases and format conventions (such as indentations). The pseudocode for the invoice entry program is shown in Fig. B-11.

Many people who code in high-level languages like COBOL and BASIC don't bother writing pseudocode. Programmers who code in assembler or machine languages frequently write their entire program in pseudocode before beginning to code in their chosen language.

The pseudocode is closer to plain English than the language used by the computer is, so it's easier to see what's happening in the processing. This is especially important when the code isn't working and needs to be debugged. Just remember, if you write pseudocode, you need to update the pseudocode whenever you make changes to your program. Otherwise, your pseudocode won't be accurate and may lead you down the proverbial primrose path when you use it as a reference.

REFERENCE MANUAL

A reference manual provides your user with information he will not need on a daily basis. This is the document where you can put the detailed tech-

```
Input "Invoice Date"
Perform Date Validation Routine
If date is 00/00/00
    GOTO Termination Routine
If date is OK
Input "Vendor ID"
Perform Vendor File Validation Routine
Input "Line Amount"
If line amount not equal to 0
    Accumulate Total
    GOTO Input Line Amount
If line amount equal to 0
    Print Accumulated total
Input "Does accumulated total match
Invoice total"
If input = N
    Perform correction routine
    GOTO Print Accumulated total
If input = Y
    Update GL file
    Update Vendor file
    Prepare Invoice Register
    GOTO Beginning of program
```

Fig. B-11. Psuedocode: invoice entry program.

nical descriptions for your programs. You can also includes lots of useful information that your user may need such as error codes, flowcharts sample screens, commands, and general start-up information, such as system installation and general sign-on procedures.

If your program is short and covers a limited scope, you may decide to collect all of your documentation into a single volume and call that a reference manual. This is acceptable, as long as the book you produce isn't so big and unwieldy that the user can't work with it. If you find that the reference manual is growing too large (physically), take the daily procedures documentation (the step-by-step procedures) and put it into a separate book.

The example shown in Fig. B-12 includes a table of contents for a typical "all-inclusive" reference manual. About the only thing that isn't included in this volume is a self-study guide. That's because self-study guides should always be packaged separately.

The first section of the manual deals with preliminary information that will be helpful to the new user. This includes a system overview, a section describing the features and benefits of the system, the equipment requirements of the system, the installation procedures, and the system checkout procedures.

The second section goes into more specific program details. It begins with a statement of general objectives of the system as a whole, but quickly advances to specific program descriptions.

The third section groups all the instructional material together in one place. The general sign-on procedures are presented first, as the user will need to know these before he can do anything else. Next, step-by-step how-to instructions for each program are given. Sticking to an optimistic approach, the program termination section talks first about normal program endings, then progresses to abnormal endings. The last section includes troubleshooting tips. As you can see, the problems the user could encounter are presented last. This arrangement of topics is chosen deliberately to convey to the user the idea that problems should be an afterthought. First, the user learns to run the programs correctly; then he learns to deal with problems.

The next section collects all of the graphics for the system. In this manual, the screen images are collected into a special section rather than being integrated with the narrative text or the step-by-step instructions. This is not to say that some screen images can't appear throughout the rest of the manual. They can and usually do. It's also help-

TABLE OF CONTENTS

Introduction

    System Overview
    Features and Benefits
    Equipment Requirements
    Installation and Set-up Procedure
    System Check Out Procedures

General Narrative

    Explanation of General Objectives
    Program Descriptions and Functions

Program Instructions

    General Sign-on Procedures
    Step-by-step Instructions for Programs
    End-Program Instructions: Normal and Abnormal
    Troubleshooting Tips

Graphics

    Sample Screens
    System Diagram
    Program Flowcharts
    Sample Reports

Messages and Commands

    Error Messages (listed alphabetically)
    Commands (listed alphabetically)

Fig. B-12. Portions of a reference manual.

SYSTEM OVERVIEW

The accounts payable module is designed to work both as a stand-alone system or in conjunction with the other BSI financial modules. Additional modules include accounts receivable, general ledger, and payroll. The accounts payable module can also be directly interfaced to both the BSI inventory control module and the BSI purchasing module.

STAND-ALONE

As a stand-alone system, the BSI accounts payable system lets you automate the tedious clerical tasks involved in invoice verification and bill-paying.

The information that appears on a vendor's invoice is entered at the time the invoice is received. This must be verified manually against the original purchase order that was issued to the vendor. If the amounts match, the information is passed to the appropriate files so that a check can be issued to the vendor. Information is also accumulated.

THE COMPLETE SYSTEM

When the accounts payable module is interfaced with the other financial, inventory, and purchasing modules available from BSI, this module forms an integral part of a complete office automation package. Purchase order information is received from the purchasing module. This information is verified against inventory receipts. When the invoice information is entered, the amounts are verified automatically and any discrepancies are reported. When the invoices are entered, the dollar amounts are automatically passed to the general ledger module. At the time actual payments are made, the appropriate general ledger accounts are automatically updated. Vendor history information is available through special inquiry programs, at the time purchase orders are generated.

FEATURES AND BENEFITS OF THE ACCOUNTS PAYABLE MODULE

The BSI accounts payable module eliminates many of the redundant clerical tasks associated with paying bills. The invoice amounts are automatically totaled and checked. Invoice amounts and payment dates are automatically kept on file and can be recovered easily. Aged balance reports are available at any time. Other reports include a preliminary check register, payment register, daily invoice report, daily payment report, and vendor history reports.

EQUIPMENT REQUIREMENTS

The BSI accounts payable module is designed to run on the QANTEL Model XXX system. If extensive record-keeping is desired, a 10mb Winchester drive is recommended.

Any of the dot-matrix or daisy wheel printers that are compatible with the QANTEL system can be used with this module.

Fig. B-12. Continued.

ful, however, to provide the user with a complete collection of every screen image he may encounter. If these screens are kept in a section by themselves, the user can turn to that section and flip through the screens until he finds the one he's looking for. This is especially helpful when a user remembers seeing a question or field name somewhere within the system, but he can't remember which module or program contained it.

The graphics section also contains the technical drawings that depict the processing flow of the system. The charts begin with a general overview chart that puts all the modules into perspective for the user. The program flowcharts are presented later. Each program flowchart may span several pages. The first page contains a high/level chart showing the subroutines that make up the program. The next few pages show the detailed processing for each of the subroutines. Usually, each routine has a page of its own. Sometimes, however, you can put two flowcharts onto a single page if they are small and simple. If you do put more than one chart onto a page (to save paper), be sure you clearly indicate that the two charts are separate and that one is not simply a continuation of the other.

Finally, samples of all the reports that are provided with the system are collected in a section. This gives the user a chance to review all of the reports and determine what information is easily obtained in printed form. It also shows the user which reports to run to get the information he wants. By providing these sample reports, you show the user what to expect on the printed page. If the report your program produces is arranged differently than the one the user is accustomed to reading, he will be prepared for the new format. You may put the totals column to the far right. His current report may put the column in the middle of the page. Of course, either way is acceptable, but your user will have to make an adjustment.

The last section of this manual provides the user with an alphabetical list of the error messages and commands found within the system. This is the type of information that isn't needed often, but when it is, the user wants to find it quickly. Even if you discuss every command and error message in your narrative, step-by-step instructions, or self-study guide, it's a good idea to repeat that information in a streamlined form. Your user won't want to wade through many pages of text to find out what a particular error message means or what command he can use to get the results he wants.

Because many of the topics listed on this table of contents are duplicated elsewhere in this appendix, only a portion of the introductory section has been reproduced here. This text shows you both the kinds of information to include and the way in which to present it.

SAMPLE REPORTS

Sample reports are actual printouts of the reports your program produces. Test or sample data is used to show the user the kind of information that is presented in the report and the format in which that information is presented.

A report sample usually cannot stand alone. You need to provide an explanation to help the user understand what he's seeing. As the report in Fig. B-13 demonstrates, every sample report should be accompanied by a brief narrative describing the information that's presented. The narrative should explain what each column is and the kind of data it contains. If you need to abbreviate words in column headings, spell them out in your narrative description. This eliminates guesswork on the part of your user and can prevent confusion.

The information contained in each column should be fully explained. If a column truncates data, explain that the report does this because of space limitations, and indicate how many characters are printed. If a vendor ID is 10 characters long, but the report shows only 6 characters, the user may be confused and wonder whether or not the report is working correctly.

Sample Report: Invoice Register

The invoice register prints the details of the invoices that are entered in a given batch. This provides a document that can be used for checking the accuracy of the figures. This register can also be kept on file for future reference.

The report sorts the invoices by invoice date, regardless of the order in which they are entered. If there are multiple invoices for a given date, these are sorted alphabetically by vendor ID. The individual line items for an invoice are printed in the order in which they were entered. The total amount of each invoice is printed in the last column on the same line as the last line item.

The first column contains the invoice date. The format for the date is MM/DD/YY. The second column contains the vendor ID. The information in these two columns is printed only once for each invoice—regardless of the number of line items.

The third column contains the amounts for the individual line items on each invoice. The amounts are listed in the order in which they were entered during invoice entry.

The total amount for each invoice is printed in the last column on the right side of the page. It appears on the same line as the last line item for the invoice.

A grand total or batch total is printed at the end of the report. This total is identified by asterisks that appear before and after the words TOTAL OF INVOICES. The actual amount appears under the last column on the right.

A single blank line is left between invoices to make it easier to read the report. A maximum of 55 lines can fit on a report page. The report will not split an invoice on a page, the report will automatically advance to the next page. The report title is printed on the first page only. Column headings and page numbers are repeated at the top of each report page.

Fig. B-13. A sample report.

INVOICE REGISTER

INVOICE DATE	VENDOR ID	ITEM AMOUNTS	TOTAL
01/01/84	ISCO	25.00	
		75.00	
		125.00	
		10.00	
		200.00	435.00
01/01/84	LITHO	35.00	35.00
01/03/84	ALLIED	20.00	
		15.00	35.00
01/05/84	HOSCO	5.00	
		10.00	
		15.00	
		10.00	
		5.00	
		25.00	70.00
01/10/84	CORBIN	175.00	175.00
01/10/84	ZACHER	80.00	
		15.00	
		10.00	105.00
******* TOTAL OF INVOICES *******			855.00

Fig. B-13. Continued.

Tell the user what will be printed when an exception condition occurs. For example, assume that your program prints a vendor report that lists the vendors alphabetically and prints the total dollar amount the vendor has received during the past year. If a vendor has not received any payments during the period, what will be printed in the dollar amount column? Will it be blank? Will it contain asterisks? Will the vendor be omitted from the list?

Your report description should also explain the order in which the records are listed. If you use multiple sorts, tell the user about all of them. Sometimes, a user thinks a report will sort records one way, when in fact, it sorts in an entirely different way. In the sample report, some users might expect the records to be sorted alphabetically by vendor ID. An equally logical assumption would be that the invoices would be printed in the order in which they were entered. The sample report in Fig. B-13 sorts the records first by invoice date. Because the invoice date is printed in the first column, it's not too difficult to determine how the records are sorted on this report. Sometimes, however, the records are sorted by information that's not printed in the first column. This is when the user can get really confused.

Most of the time, your sample reports will be no more than one page in length. It's important to tell your user what happens when his report must overflow to a second page. He needs to know whether or not the title and column headings are repeated on each page of the report, and whether or not the pages are numbered sequentially. He also needs to know what happens to the records. Some reports put breaks after certain records. For example, if you were printing a mailing list for club members from around the country, you might group the records by state. You could force each state listing to begin on a new page. Some reports split records across pages. If the record is too long to fit onto a single page, the report prints as many lines as it can and then prints the next line on the next

page. No matter how your report handles information, it's essential to tell your user what to expect.

SCREEN IMAGES

The old saying, "a picture is worth a thousand words" certainly applies to program documentation. You can spend pages upon pages of text trying to explain what the user will see when he looks at a particular screen. Some users will be able to visualize the screen image quickly. Others will not be able to grasp what you're describing until they see the actual screen.

If a user can't visualize what a screen will look like, it will be hard to understand your instructions and explanations. You can eliminate this problem by using screen images to show your user what he will see when he runs your program. Figures B-14 and B-15 show screen images from the invoice entry program.

Your screen images can be photographs or line drawings. Some systems even give you the opportunity of printing your screens. Whichever technique you use, be sure your screen image contains meaningful information.

Many people show data entry screens in their pure form, with no data on them. They may look clean and uncluttered to you but they won't be very helpful to your user. Your user may not be sure of the kind of data he's supposed to enter on the screen or how many characters he can put in each field. If you fill in the fields with sample data, your user will have a better idea of the information he'll need to

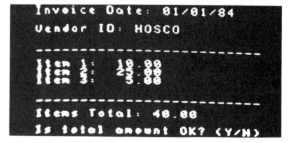

Fig. B-14. A screen shot from the invoice entry program.

180

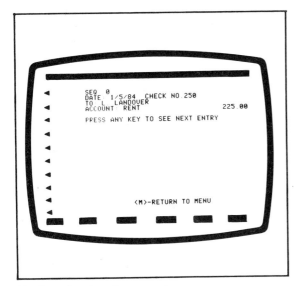

```
        SEQ  0
        DATE  1/5/84   CHECK NO 250
        TO  L  LANDOVER
        ACCOUNT  RENT                  225.00

        PRESS ANY KEY TO SEE NEXT ENTRY




                  <M>-RETURN TO MENU
```

Fig. B-15. Drawing of a screen image.

enter on the screen. A compromise between the pure screen and the screen with test data is to show a screen that gives the user an idea of the information that's required without showing him sample data. Instead of putting sample data in the fields on the screen, put asterisks or Xs in the alphanumeric fields and 9s in the numeric fields. This will tell your user the kind of information that can be put in each field as well as the maximum number of characters that will fit in a field.

SELF-STUDY GUIDE

A self-study guide serves as a teacher for new users. When you can't go to every customer's home or office and give private or group lessons, a self-study guide is a must. If the guide is written correctly, the user should feel almost as comfortable working with it as he would working with you.

The sample excerpt from a self-study guide in Fig. B-16 shows how the operating procedures for a single program are taught to the user.

The first section introduces the new user to the program and tries to draw parallels between the automated system and the more familiar manual system. Because test data was provided with the package, the user is told that he will be working with specially provided test vendors. This prepares the user to see unfamiliar IDs and reassures him that he will be playing with test data rather than with real data.

The first example walks the user through the basic processing steps of the program. Entries that can cause confusion (such as the data format) are explained so the user will understand what is expected of him. The first example stresses the positive side of the processing. The user is forced to complete the invoice whether or not his total is correct.

The second example reinforces what was taught in the first example. It allows the user to test his wings and try entering some information on his own. Again, the user is forced to complete the invoice entry whether the total is correct or not.

The third example shows the user how to correct mistakes. By this point, the user should be feeling comfortable with the general operations of the program. Because new material is introduced in this example, the user is walked through the new technique.

The fourth example covers entirely new material. It shows the user how to exit from the program correctly. The user is hand-held through the termination process so that he will feel comfortable with it.

The basic procedures for running the invoice entry program are shown in the four examples. A sample invoice is used to give the user a sense of what it will be like to take a printed document and transfer the information to the computer.

The last section of this lesson contains practice exercises. These are designed to help the user become more familiar with the processing. The

Self-Study Guide: Invoice Entry Program

The acounts payable system lets you write checks and pay vendor invoices automatically. Like your bookkeeper, the system needs to know a few facts before it can issue checks to vendors. Most of the information the system needs can be found on the paper invoices the vendors send you.

In order for the computer to help you with your bill payment, you need to give it the information it needs. The invoice entry program lets you take the information from the invoices the vendors send you and put it into the system.

In this lesson, you'll learn how to run the invoice entry program. The system is supplied with two fictitious vendors that you can use in the following exercises. When you actually run this program to enter your company's invoices, you'll need to be sure that your vendor file has been built so that you can use valid vendor IDs.

EXERCISE 1

Choose the INVOICE ENTRY (IE) program from the main menu. The first thing you will see on the screen is the prompt INVOICE DATE:

For this example, we'll use January 5, 1984 as our date. To enter this date, type 01/05/84. Press the RETURN key after you've typed in the date.

Next, the prompt VENDOR ID: appears on the screen. We'll pretend the invoice came from a vendor whose ID is TEST. Type the word TEST; then press the RETURN key.

The system then asks you to enter the dollar amount of the first line item. Type in 10.00. You don't need to put a dollar sign ($) before the amount. Press the RETURN key after you've typed the amount.

The system is now ready for you to type in the dollar amount of the next line item. Type in 20.00; then press the RETURN key.

When the system prompts you to enter the third dollar amount, type in 00 and press the RETURN key. The 00 tells the system that you don't have any more line items to enter.

The total amount for all the line items you entered is displayed and should be 30.00. The system will prompt you to verify this amount and say whether or not it is correct. Type a Y in the space provided.

You're now back at the beginning. The system is ready for you to begin entering the next invoice. You have successfully entered an invoice.

EXAMPLE 2

Lets say you ordered several packets of seeds from the Little Hooters Seed

Fig. B-16. A self-study guide.

Company. When the invoice arrives, you need to enter the figures into the system. Your company's vendor ID for the Little Hooters Seed Company is LHSC. Here's what the invoice from the company looks like:

LITTLE HOOTERS SEED COMPANY

INVOICE

02/08/84

1	Packet	Big Orange Carrot Seeds	1.00
1	Packet	Decorative Red Lace Kale	2.00
1	Packet	Indian Corn Seeds	1.50
2	Packets	Tom Thumb Tomato Seeds	2.50
1	Packet	Emerald Green Peppers	1.25
1	Packet	Butter & Sugar Corn	1.75
1	Packet	Invisible Beans	1.00
		Total Amount:	11.00

To enter the information from this invoice into the system, you need to follow the same procedure that was described in Example 1. We've already noted that the vendor ID is LHSC. The vendor has even done you the favor of putting the date into the right format. Try entering the rest of the information on your own to get the feel of entering an invoice. After you've entered the price for the invisible beans, you should enter 00 as the next amount. The system will then total the line item amounts and show you the total amount for the invoice. If the total is not $11.00, check your figures. Did you make a mistake? If you did, don't worry about correcting it for now. Just answer the question with a Y.

EXAMPLE 3

In this example, you will learn how to correct mistakes. Lets use the Little Hooters Seed Company invoice again.

Enter the invoice just as you did before, only this time, type 5.00 for the price of the invisible beans. The total will be 15.00.

Fig. B-16. Continued.

Though the system performed its arithmetic correctly, the total doesn't agree with the total on your printed invoice. A quick glance over the line item figures shows you that the invisible beans entry is the culprit.

To correct your mistakes, type an N as your answer to whether or not the total amount is correct. The system will take you back to the first line item and show you the figure you typed. If that figure is correct, (which we know it is) press the RETURN key. The system will then show you the next line item amount. Keep pressing the RETURN key until you reach the item that needs to be corrected.

When you get to the invisible beans line, type 1.00 over the 5.00 that is displayed; then press the RETURN key. The system will then display the OO line. Press the RETURN key again, and the system will recompute the total.

Now that your invoice entry has been corrected, you can answer Y to the last question on the screen.

EXAMPLE 4

You've now had practice entering invoices. Let's pretend that that's all the invoices you have to enter. You need to tell the system that you're finished. To do this, type OO/OO/OO as the date when the next date prompt is displayed. When you press the RETURN key, the system will see the date you've typed and automatically know that you're done. A message appears on the screen that asks you, PRINT INVOICE REGISTER?

An invoice register is a printed report that contains the details of the invoices you've just entered. To print this report, be sure that you have paper in your printer and that the printer is turned on. Type a Y in answer to the question; then press the RETURN key. The report will be printed automatically.

You don't have to print the report. If you answer N to the question, the report won't be printed. The invoice register report can only be printed immediately after you've entered a batch of invoices. Once you say No and exit from the program, you won't be able to print the report.

If you ask to have the report printed, a message will be displayed on the screen saying INVOICE REGISTER BEING PRINTED ... PLEASE WAIT. When the report has been printed, you are returned to the main menu. If you decide not to print the register, the system takes you immediately to the main menu.

PRACTICE EXERCISES

Now that you know how to enter and correct invoices, and how to print an invoice register, you should have no trouble entering these invoices.

Fig. B-16. Continued.

LITTLE HOOTER SEED COMPANY

Invoice
01/17/84

1	Bag	Special Grade A Mulch	7.50
1	Dozen	Peat Pots#3	3.50

Total: 11.00

LITTLE HOOTER SEED COMPANY

Invoice
01/27/84

1	Packet	Sweet and Early Peas	1.50
1	Packet	Bright and Colorful Zinnia Seeds	1.50
1	Plant	Pink & Blue Rosebush	7.00
1	Packet	Yarrow Seeds	1.25
1	Book	How to Grow Flowers	8.75

Total: 20.00

LITTLE HOOTER SEED COMPANY

INVOICE
02/10/84

1	Kit	Kitchen Herb Garden	15.75
1	Dozen	Tomato Frames	36.00
1	Flat	Gentle Giant Tomatoes	FREE

Total: 51.75

Fig. B-16. Continued.

```
                    LITTLE HOOTER SEED COMPANY

                             INVOICE
                            01/13/84

    1    Box       Special Formula Fertilizer                FREE
    1    Plant     Royal Crimson African Violet              3.25
    1    Plant     Purple Passion African Violet             3.25
    1    Plant     Delicate Pink African Violet              3.25
    1    Packet    Funny Face Pumpkin Seeds                  1.25

                   Total:                                   11.00
```

If you've completed the examples successfully, you know how to enter invoices. Did you get caught on the last invoice? If you typed 00 as the amount for the first line, you got a total of 00. This is because the system thought you were done with that invoice, and it totaled the line items you entered—a grand total of 00!

Whenever an invoice shows a free or no charge item, skip that line you enter the invoice. The system is only concerned with the items you need to pay for. It doesn't care about the ones you get for free.

Did you print an invoice register for the batch of invoices you just entered? If you didn't you should practice entering them again and print the report this time.

Fig. B-16. Continued.

length of the invoices is varied to increase the probability that the user will make a typing mistake that will need to be corrected.

The second-to-the-last example sets the user up for the trick in the last invoice. By putting the FREE item at the end of the example, the user can get away with putting 00 as the amount. In the last example, however, the user is tripped up if he tries to put 00 as the amount for the first line item. The explanation following the practice examples addresses this anticipated problem. It doesn't scold users who were caught in the trap. Instead, it acknowledges that, indeed, there was a trap deliberately set. A full explanation of why the FREE item was included and how to handle similar situations with real invoices is included.

The user is also asked whether or not he elected to print the invoice register. If he did not, he's encouraged (but not forced) to repeat the exercise and print the report.

While this may seem like a very long lesson for such a seemingly simple program, you can see that each example was carefully chosen. The user is very slowly and deliberately walked from the first introduction to the program through the proper ending of the program. As old material is mastered, new material is introduced. The practice exercises at the end of the lesson are designed to test the user's ability to run the program. The last exercise is designed to get the user thinking about what he's doing. Because the program is simple, the user can quickly become drone-like in his operation. By putting a trap into the last exercise, the guide reminds the user that he must be on his toes even when running simple programs.

PROGRAM SPECIFICATIONS

Program specifications are the instructions given to a programmer that enable him to properly code the program so that it works the way it's supposed to and performs the tasks required of it.

Any programmer should be able to read your program specifications and know exactly how to write code that meets the needs of the program. Your specifications should include file descriptions, a logic narrative, screen mockups, and report mockups.

The file descriptions should not only list the fields that belong in each file, they should also describe the characteristics of each field. The characteristics include the length of each field and the type of data it will accept.

The programming logic consists of three elements. First, there is the main or iterative logic of the program. Second, there are the subroutines that are called during the main logic processing. Third, there are the validation routines. These three elements can be arranged in any order. In the sample specification in Fig. B-17, the validation routines are described first, the main processing logic is next, and the subroutines are described last. Notice that each element is clearly identified and separated from the others.

Be very specific when you write the logic requirements of the main processing, the validations, and the subroutines. If you omit any special condi-

tions and the processing for them, that logic will be omitted from the program and unanticipated problems may result.

Screen and report mockups are essential elements of a program specification. They show the programmer where to put the prompts and messages that are to be displayed and how to set up a report. If you don't show your coder where to position the various pieces of information, you may be surprised and disappointed with the results. The sample mockups were prepared on a word processor with 80 column margins. These mockups provide guidelines for positioning the information. If you want to be more precise, you can use specially designed sheets of paper that look something like graph paper. This paper comes in pads and is available commercially in 80, 132, and 150 column widths. The columns are numbered at the top of each sheet so you can position each letter exactly. Use pencil when you're preparing your mockup screens and reports—and keep an eraser handy. You'll probably need to try several arrangements before you're satisfied with the way the mockup looks.

When you prepare a screen or report mockup, you need to show the coder (and yourself) what the screen or report will look like with data. Use the number 9 to represent numeric data and the letter X to represent alphanumeric data. Always fill each field to its maximum size so you'll know if you've left enough room horizontally for all the information. Ideally, you should center the information on the screen or report page. If this technique doesn't seem to work well with a particular screen or report, left-justify the information so that there is a straight line of starting points on the left side of the screen. When you do attempt to center information, be precise. There's nothing more annoying and distracting to a user than an off-balance screen.

If you are both the designer and coder, you should still consider preparing a detailed program specification. Many times, you'll find that as you are

Specifications: Invoice Entry Program
              BSI Accounts Payable System

Purpose of the Program:

   This program is used to transfer invoice details from printed vendor invoices to the system. The data is then transferred to the vendor file, the general file (if the interface is active) and a printed report called the Invoice Register.

File Description:

   The invoice entry file contains the following fields with the described characteristics.

Invoice Date	8 characters alphanumeric
Vendor ID	6 characters alphanumeric
Line Item Amounts (max 25)	7 characters numeric
Total Amount	9 characters numeric
Is Total Correct	1 character (Y or N)

Validations:

Date Validation: A standard date validation must be invoked to insure that the month field is greater than 0 and less than 13. The day field for months 04, 06, 09, and 11 must not be greater than 30. The day field for month 02 must not exceed 29. The day field for all other months must not exceed 31. The year field must be checked for numeric data. If any of the data in the data entry is invalid, a buzz should sound and the user should not be permitted to advance to another field. If the date that is entered is equal to 00 00 00, the termination routine is invoked.

Vendor ID Validation: The vendor ID that is entered should be validated against the vendor ID field in the vendor file. If a match is not found, a buzz should sound and the user should not be permitted to advance to another field.

Processing Logic:

   Begin the processing by clearing all fields and zeroing out the total accumulator. The user is to enter data one field at a time. The first field that is displayed is the date field. When the date is entered, the date validation routine must be called. If the date value is accepted, the prompt for entry of the vendor ID is displayed. When the vendor ID is displayed, the vendor ID validation routine must

Fig. B-17. Program specifications.

be called and the vendor file must be read. If the vendor ID data is valid, the prompt for the first line item amount is displayed. The user enters numeric data. The value that is entered is added to a total accumulator. Up to 25 line item amounts can be entered. After the user has entered 25 line item amounts, the total amount for the items should be displayed along with the following message:

LINE ITEM ENTRIES MAY NOT EXCEED 25. CHECK TOTAL AMOUNT FOR ABOVE ENTRIES. REMAINING LINE ITEM AMOUNTS MUST BE ENTERED ON SEPARATE INVOICE ENTRY.

As each line item amount is entered, it must be checked. If the amount is equal to 00, the total amount to be displayed on the screen. When the total amount is entered on the screen, the following prompt is displayed:

Does total amount equal invoice total? (Y/N).

The user must enter a Y or an N. If any other value is entered, a buzz should sound and the user should not be allowed to advance. If the answer is Y, add the total amount to the vendor YTD accumulator in the vendor file. Check to see if the GL interface is active, and if it is, add the amount to the A/P pending field. Write the entire invoice record to the invoice file. Advance to the next invoice and repeat the process. If the answer is N, the correction routine should be invoked.

Correction Routine:

The correction routine begins by zeroing out the total accumulator. The correction routine then displays the first line item amount. When the user presses the RETURN key, add the amount in the field to the total accumulator and display the next line item amount. The user may strikeover the numbers in the amount field. The line item amounts are displayed one-by-one until either the maximum number of entries (25) is reached, or the 00 amount is entered. The total is then displayed and processing continues as described in the main processing logic section.

Termination Routine:

The screen is cleared except for the prompt:

Do you want to print an Invoice Register (Y/N)?

If the answer is Y, call the invoice register routine and print the report; then return the display to the main menu. If the answer is N, return the display to the main menu.

Fig. B-17. Continued.

Invoice Register Routine:

Display the following message on the screen:

INVOICE REGISTER IN PROGRESS ... PLEASE WAIT.

Sort the invoice file by date in ascending order. If two or more dates are the same, sort the records alphabetically by vendor ID in ascending order. The report is formatted like the sample report mock-up.

SCREEN MOCKUPS

Screen 1: Invoice Entry

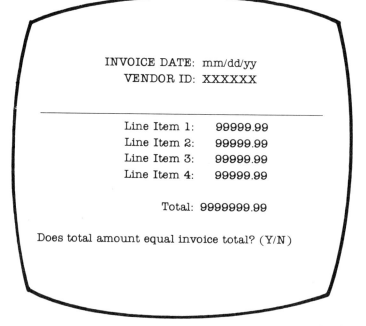

```
          INVOICE DATE: mm/dd/yy
            VENDOR ID: XXXXXX
      _____

            Line Item 1:    99999.99
            Line Item 2:    99999.99
            Line Item 3:    99999.99
            Line Item 4:    99999.99

              Total: 9999999.99

      Does total amount equal invoice total? (Y/N)
```

Fig. B-17. Continued.

190

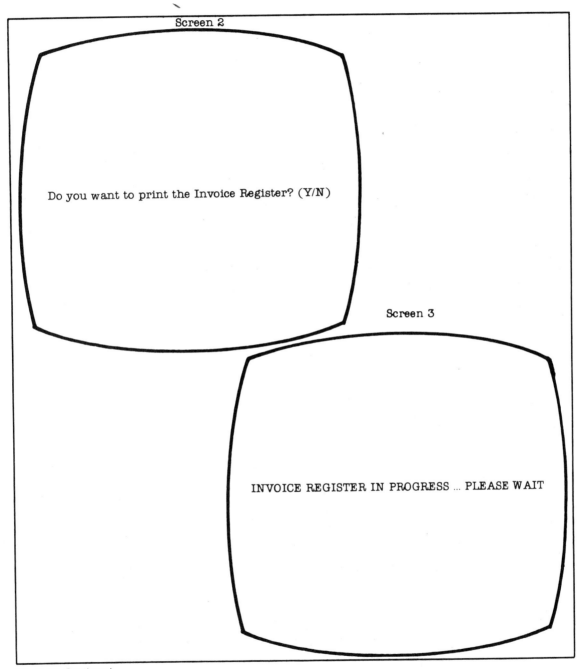

Screen 2

Do you want to print the Invoice Register? (Y/N)

Screen 3

INVOICE REGISTER IN PROGRESS ... PLEASE WAIT

Fig. B-17. Continued.

```
                          INVOICE REGISTER

     INVOICE DATE          VENDOR ID          ITEM AMOUNTS          TOTAL

        mm/dd/yy            XXXXXX               99999.99
                                                 99999.99
                                                 99999.99
                                                 99999.99
                                                 99999.99             9999999.99

        mm/dd/yy            XXXXXX               99999.99             9999999.99

        mm/dd/yy            XXXXXX               99999.99
                                                 99999.99             9999999.99

        mm/dd/yy            XXXXXX               99999.99
                                                 99999.99
                                                 99999.99
                                                 99999.99
                                                 99999.99
                                                 99999.99             9999999.99

        mm/dd/yy            XXXXXX               99999.99             9999999.99

        mm/dd/yy            XXXXXX               99999.99
                                                 99999.99
                                                 99999.99             9999999.99

     ******* TOTAL OF INVOICES *******                               9999999.99
```

Fig. B-17. Continued.

writing the logic narrative, you think of things you overlooked. For example, if you were writing the sample specification, you might know that you needed to enter the line items and get a total, but you might forget to set up a special accumulator area to collect the amounts. The act of writing a detailed specification forces you to think through the logic of your program. By including screen and report mockups, you have the opportunity to plan the layout of the information. If you jump right into the coding, you may get some ugly screens and reports.

STEP-BY-STEP INSTRUCTIONS

Step-by-step instructions are designed to lead the user through the interactive processing steps of a program. This kind of documentation is designed to let the user complete the activities of a program—whether or not he understands fully what he is doing or why he is doing it.

Think of this type of documentation in the context of an office. The sample instructions in Fig. B-18 are for the invoice entry program. Normally, you would have a staff member assigned to run the program and enter the invoice information into the computer. What happens if that employee is on vacation or out sick? Somebody has to enter the invoice information. The office manager either asks another staff member to help out or brings in temporary help. In either case, the person who is assigned to enter the invoices is probably not familiar with the program. In fact, that person may not even understand much about the whole area of accounts payable and invoices.

Well written step-by-step instructions will enable the stand-in to get the invoices entered with minimal instruction and help from the manager.

Step-by-step instructions should be numbered sequentially and the steps should be listed in the order in which they are performed. List one instruction with each number.

Because the instructions are more how-to than why instructions, you don't need to give lengthy explanations for why things occur. You simply need to state what the user will see and what will happen visually as a result of the user's actions.

You'll note that in the sample instructions, some brief explanations are supplied. This is done to help give the user a basic understanding of what's going on when he runs the program. For example, if

---

Step-by-Step Instructions: Invoice Entry Program

1. Choose the Invoice Entry (IE) program from the main menu by typing IE in the space provided and pressing the RETURN key.

2. Type in the invoice date using the format mm/dd/yy; then press the RETURN key. The date you enter should be the date on which the vendor issued the invoice—not the date you received it, or the date on which you are entering it.

3. Type in the 6-character ID you have assigned to the vendor and press the RETURN key. The ID you enter will be checked against the vendor file. If you are entering an invoice for a new vendor and there is no record yet on file, you must create a vendor record before you can enter the invoice.

4. Enter the dollar amount of the first line item on the invoice. Be sure to include the decimal point and the cents figures. Do not include the dollar sign ($). Press the RETURN key.

5. Continue to enter the dollar amounts of the line items until you have no more amounts to enter. When the prompt is displayed for another line, type 00 as the amount, and press the RETURN key.

6. The system will display the total amount of all the line amounts that have been entered. Check this amount against the total printed on the vendor invoice.

Fig. B-18. Step-by-step instructions.

7. The system will ask you if the two totals agree. If they do, type a Y in the space provided. The system will then let you enter the next invoice.

8. If the two totals do not agree, type an N in the space provided. You will then have the opportunity to change the amounts of any line items and add new line items.

9. As each item amount is displayed, press the RETURN key if the amount is correct. Type the correct amount over the old amount when you find an error When you've entered all the amounts, type 00 as the amount.

10. The system will then display the new total and again ask you if it is correct.

11. When all of the invoices have been entered, type 00/00/00 as the date on the next invoice entry screen. This tells the system that you've finished entering the batch of invoices.

12. A new screen is displayed. The question "Do you want to print an Invoice Register?" is asked. Type a Y to print the report. Type a N to skip the report.

13. If you decide to print the report, the system will display a message telling you that the register printing is in progress. When the report has finished printing, the main menu screen is displayed.

14. If you do not print the invoice register, the system will immediately display the main menu.

Fig. B-18. Continued.

a new user tries to enter an invoice for a new vendor, he'll get a buzz sound when the invoice validation takes place. The new user looks at the invoice and checks his typing of the ID; everything looks okay. If a brief explanation hadn't been supplied to tell the user that the vendor must exist on the vendor file first, the user might think the program wasn't working properly.

The best test for step-by-step instructions is to hand them to a new user and see if he can run through the entire program. If so, bravo! If not, change the instructions that are confusing or incomplete.

Glossary of Terms

active voice—verb construction that shows direct action (for example, Jack hits Sam).

analysts—people who identify problems and needs, and then seek and develop programming solutions.

annotated listing—a program listing that has been embellished with handwritten or encoded notes.

block diagram—a chart using rectangles to represent information.

boldface—letters that are printed darker in appearance than the surrounding text.

bugs—coding deficiencies that cause the program to work differently from the way it was designed to work.

code—words and symbols that are grouped and structured according to the conventions of a particular programming language.

command keys—preprogrammed keys that let the user execute a specific command (for example, RETURN, TAB, CONTROL)

comment section—a paragraph contained in a program that conveys information to the programmer and is not processed when the program is run.

control—the processing activity that takes place when a program is run.

copyright—a legal form of protection for the author of an original work such as a program or documentation.

copyright notice—a visible announcement of copyright ownership that complies with the formats outlined by copyright laws.

data—information that is input to or produced by a program.

data dictionary—an alphabetical list of the terms a user needs to know in order to run a program. The definitions for these terms are specific to the program.

detailed outline—an outline of the topics, subtopics, and facts to be included in a documentation narrative.

development programmers—individuals who create programs based on information supplied to them by analysts.

documentation—a written explanation of what programs do, how they relate to one another, and how they work.

dot matrix printer—a printer that forms letters, characters, and symbols using dot patterns.

enhancements—modifications to a program that improve its performance or capabilities and were not included in the original design specifications.

error messages—text that is displayed on the screen or on a printout that signals that an error condition has been encountered during processing.

file description—a table containing the names of all the data fields that belong to a file and the sizes and characteristics of each field.

flowchart—a graphic representation of the coding logic of a program or subroutine using a standardized set of symbols.

graph paper—paper that has preprinted horizontal and vertical lines that form squares that are sized to a specific scale.

growling words—words with phonetically unpleasant sounds that disturb a reader.

input file—information that is fed to a program from a previously stored file.

italics—letters printed with a diagonal slant rather than a perpendicular one.

linguistics—the study of language as a science.

logic list—a list of the logical steps or procedures required to successfully complete a predefined task programmatically.

maintenance programmer—a programmer who works with existing programs to correct, modify, and enhance the code.

module—a group of related subroutines or programs that accomplish a well-defined task.

output file—a group of related fields that are created as a result of program processing. This file may be stored within the system or printed.

paragraph—a group of related sentences that convey information about a single topic.

passive voice—a verb construction that shows indirect action (for example, Sam was hit by Jack).

photostat—a black and white photographic reproduction made with a specially designed camera that provides high contrast, accurate reproduction of details, and a variety of reduction or enlargement sizes.

problem statement—a detailed description of a problem that can be solved programmatically. The statement includes all the conditions that must be addressed in order to accomplish a particular task.

program—a subroutine or group of related subroutines that perform a predefined task.

program listing—a printed copy of the code that is used in a program.

program narrative—documentation that provides an overview of what a program does, a high level description of how it works, and a statement of the problems it is designed to solve. A program narrative may also describe special hardware, software, or data requirements of the program.

programmable keys—special keys that can be accessed and made operative for special functions using program code. These keys are also called soft keys, smart keys, program function keys, and function keys. The functions these keys perform can vary from program to program or within a single program.

pseudocode—an English translation of the code that is used to create a program. Pseudocode does not have to adhere to syntax rules that apply to code.

publisher—an individual or business that prints and distributes text and software.

readability—a means of measuring text to determine the level of difficulty the syntax, sentence length, and vocabulary will pose to a reader.

reference manual—a written document providing technical information pertaining to the operation and functioning of a program or system.

REM—a BASIC statement that precedes comment text. Information following this statement will not be processed.

rough draft—a narrative text written from a detailed outline that is the writer's first attempt at translating the outline into complete sentences. The focus of the writer is usually on content rather than style.

royalties—compensation paid to an author by a publisher. This type of compensation is a percentage of the price of the author's work and the amount is dependent upon the number of copies that the publisher can sell.

sample reports—printed reports using test data to show how a report will look when generated by a program.

screen image—a photograph or line drawing of a screen that is displayed when a program is run.

screen messages—text displayed on the screen that provides the program user with information, prompts, and warnings.

second person writing—text which uses the pronoun *you* as the primary subject of its sentences.

sentence—a group of words that expresses a complete thought, idea, concept, or fact. To qualify as a sentence, the group of words must conform to the standard rules of grammar, syntax, and punctuation.

self-study guide—written program documentation that is presented in a sequence that permits the reader to learn proper operating procedures without the need for classroom or individual instruction.

soothing words—words with phonetically pleasing sounds that relax the reader.

specifications—a set of instructions designed to show a programmer the conditions, limitations, and logic required to code a program.

step-by-step instructions—program operating instructions that are designed to let the reader walk-through the execution of a program one step at a time.

subroutine—a group of related lines of code designed to perform a single specifically defined task.

symbols—shapes and characters used on charts to express programming logic.

synonyms—words having the same or very similar meanings. Words that are synonyms can be substituted for one another in text.

system—a group of related programs or modules that perform the tasks required to solve a large-scale problem.

technical documentation—documentation that is written for programmers and explains how the logic of a program works.

template—a graphic tool made out of thin cardboard or plastic that is used to draw specific shapes of specific sizes.

test data—data that is supplied with a program to allow the user to experiment with the program operation. Test data closely resembles the actual information the user will use when running the program to perform its stated application.

third person writing—text that uses terms like *the user* and pronouns like he, she, and they.

tone—the general emotional feeling created by a block of text.

topic sentence—the key sentence in a paragraph that summarizes the objective of the paragraph.

type style—the physical appearance of a printed alphabet set.

user—a person who uses a program to perform the task for which it was designed. In some cases, the user may be a programmer who incorporates a program or subroutine into his own code.

user documentation—written documentation that explains how to run a program and what tasks the program can perform.

Users' Group—a group of people with a common computer-related interest. In some cases, the individuals own the same brand of computer; in other cases, the group is made up of programmers coding in the same language.

utility—a program that is designed to efficiently solve a system operations problem or a coding problem.

vanity press—a publisher who prints copies of software and text at the author's expense.

variable list—an alphabetical list of the variables that are used in the code for a program as well as the definitions and characteristics of these variables.

Index